W9-AVK-653

Women in the
Military

POINT COUNTERPOINT

SEVERNA PARK HIGH SCHOOL
20130002217
355.008 SHE
Women in the military

Women in the Military

Victoria Sherrow

SERIES CONSULTING EDITOR
Alan Marzilli, M.A., J.D.

SEVERNA PARK HIGH SCHOOL
MEDIA CENTER

CHELSEA HOUSE
PUBLISHERS
An imprint of Infobase Publishing

Women in the Military

Copyright © 2007 by Infobase Publishing

All rights reserved. No part of this book may be reproduced or utilized in any form or by any means, electronic or mechanical, including photocopying, recording, or by any information storage or retrieval systems, without permission in writing from the publisher. For information, contact:

Chelsea House
An imprint of Infobase Publishing
132 West 31st Street
New York, NY 10001

Library of Congress Cataloging-in-Publication Data

Sherrow, Victoria.
  Women in the military / Victoria Sherrow.
      p. cm. — (Point/counterpoint)
  Includes bibliographical references and index.
  ISBN-13: 978-0-7910-9290-3 (hardcover)
  ISBN-10: 0-7910-9290-9 (hardcover)
  1. Women soldiers—United States. 2. United States—Armed Forces—Women.
I. Title. II. Series.

  UB418.W65S46 2007
  355.0082'0973—dc22   2007001836

Chelsea House books are available at special discounts when purchased in bulk quantities for businesses, associations, institutions, or sales promotions. Please call our Special Sales Department in New York at (212) 967-8800 or (800) 322-8755.

You can find Chelsea House on the World Wide Web at
http://www.chelseahouse.com

Series and cover design by Takeshi Takahashi

Printed in the United States of America

Bang Hermitage 10 9 8 7 6 5 4 3 2 1

This book is printed on acid-free paper.

All links and Web addresses were checked and verified to be correct at the time of publication. Because of the dynamic nature of the Web, some addresses and links may have changed since publication and may no longer be valid.

CONTENTS

Foreword
Alan Marzilli, M.A., J.D.
Washington, D.C.

The debates presented in POINT/COUNTERPOINT are among the most interesting and controversial in contemporary American society, but studying them is more than an academic activity. They affect every citizen; they are the issues that today's leaders debate and tomorrow's will decide. The reader may one day play a central role in resolving them.

Why study both sides of the debate? It's possible that the reader will not yet have formed any opinion at all on the subject of this volume—but this is unlikely. It is more likely that the reader will already hold an opinion, probably a strong one, and very probably one formed without full exposure to the arguments of the other side. It is rare to hear an argument presented in a balanced way, and it is easy to form an opinion on too little information; these books will help to fill in the informational gaps that can never be avoided. More important, though, is the practical function of the series: Skillful argumentation requires a thorough knowledge of *both* sides—though there are seldom only two, and only by knowing what an opponent is likely to assert can one form an articulate response.

Perhaps more important is that listening to the other side sometimes helps one to see an opponent's arguments in a more human way. For example, Sister Helen Prejean, one of the nation's most visible opponents of capital punishment, has been deeply affected by her interactions with the families of murder victims. Seeing the families' grief and pain, she understands much better why people support the death penalty, and she is able to carry out her advocacy with a greater sensitivity to the needs and beliefs of those who do not agree with her. Her relativism, in turn, lends credibility to her work. Dismissing the other side of the argument as totally without merit can be too easy—it is far more useful to understand the nature of the controversy and the reasons *why* the issue defies resolution.

The most controversial issues of all are often those that center on a constitutional right. The Bill of Rights—the first ten amendments to the U.S. Constitution—spells out some of the most fundamental rights that distinguish the governmental system of the United States from those that allow fewer (or other) freedoms. But the sparsely worded document is open to interpretation, and clauses of only a few words are often at the heart of national debates. The Bill of Rights was meant to protect individual liberties; but the needs of some individuals clash with those of society as a whole, and when this happens someone has to decide where to draw the line. Thus the Constitution becomes a battleground between the rights of individuals to do as they please and the responsibility of the government to protect its citizens. The First Amendment's guarantee of "freedom of speech," for example, leads to a number of difficult questions. Some forms of expression, such as burning an American flag, lead to public outrage—but nevertheless are said to be protected by the First Amendment. Other types of expression that most people find objectionable, such as sexually explicit material involving children, are not protected because they are considered harmful. The question is not only where to draw the line, but how to do this without infringing on the personal liberties on which the United States was built.

The Bill of Rights raises many other questions about individual rights and the societal "good." Is a prayer before a high school football game an "establishment of religion" prohibited by the First Amendment? Does the Second Amendment's promise of "the right to bear arms" include concealed handguns? Is stopping and frisking someone standing on a corner known to be frequented by drug dealers a form of "unreasonable search and seizure" in violation of the Fourth Amendment? Although the nine-member U.S. Supreme Court has the ultimate authority in interpreting the Constitution, its answers do not always satisfy the public. When a group of nine people—sometimes by a five-to-four vote—makes a decision that affects the lives of hundreds of millions, public outcry can be expected. And the composition of the Court does change over time, so even a landmark decision is not guaranteed to stand forever. The limits of constitutional protection are always in flux.

These issues make headlines, divide courts, and decide elections. They are the questions most worthy of national debate, and this series aims to cover them as thoroughly as possible. Each volume sets out some of the key arguments surrounding a particular issue, even some views that most people consider extreme or radical—but presents a balanced perspective on the issue. Excerpts from the relevant laws and judicial opinions and references to central concepts, source material, and advocacy groups help the reader to explore the issues even further and to read "the letter of the law" just as the legislatures and the courts have established it.

It may seem that some debates—such as those over capital punishment and abortion, debates with a strong moral component— will never be resolved. But American history offers numerous examples of controversies that once seemed insurmountable but now are effectively settled, even if only on the surface. Abolitionists met with widespread resistance to their efforts to end slavery, and the controversy over that issue threatened to cleave the nation in two; but today public debate over the merits of slavery would be unthinkable, though racial inequalities still plague the nation. Similarly unthinkable at one time was suffrage for women and minorities, but this is now a matter of course. Distributing information about contraception once was a crime. Societies change, and attitudes change, and new questions of social justice are raised constantly while the old ones fade into irrelevancy.

Whatever the root of the controversy, the books in POINT/ COUNTERPOINT seek to explain to the reader the origins of the debate, the current state of the law, and the arguments on both sides. The goal of the series is to inform the reader about the issues facing not only American politicians, but all of the nation's citizens, and to encourage the reader to become more actively involved in resolving these debates, as a voter, a concerned citizen, a journalist, an activist, or an elected official. Democracy is based on education, and every voice counts—so every opinion must be an informed one.

Questions about the role of women in the armed forces are particularly relevant today. As the conflict in Iraq continues to consume resources, the U.S. military is looking for ways to increase enlistment. This volume begins with a look at the history of female military service up to the present day, followed by an examination of an extremely controversial issue: whether women should be assigned to ground combat. With more women being placed in harm's way in Iraq, the issue has generated renewed debate. Included in the discussion of ground combat duty are some underlying philosophical discussions about the role of women in society and inherent physical and psychological differences between men and women. Two additional topics examined at length are gender-integrated training and units and the armed forces' policies regarding motherhood.

Changing Roles for Women

In January 1990, 29-year-old Linda L. Bray made history when she led a mixed-gender company in a combat situation. As commander of the 988th Military Police Company during the U.S. invasion of Panama, Bray crashed through a gate in her Army jeep in an operation to secure a K-9 compound. Her company, which included 15 men and 15 women, encountered enemy snipers. Bray used her 9mm pistol as her group returned fire. Inside the compound, they found attack dogs, weapons used by hostile troops from the Panamanian Defense Force (PDF), and items that yielded intelligence information. They took one prisoner, and three dead PDF soldiers were found near the compound.

When the media began coverage of this story, the American audience reacted strongly. To some, Bray's experience showed that women had "the right stuff" and could fight alongside men.

Other people were outraged that a woman had come face to face with enemy troops and had fired a weapon. Some objected to women commanding men. Army officials declared that the women in Bray's company were not actually in ground combat units, which is not allowed by Pentagon rules. During the months that followed, questions arose as to whether or not Bray's company had killed the three PDF soldiers and how long the fighting really lasted. A Pentagon correspondent claimed that the battle and Bray's role in it had been "grossly exaggerated."[1]

The discussion and media coverage of the Panama incident reflected long-standing disagreements about women in the military—as well as women's roles in general. Since the 1940s, these roles have changed dramatically as women have entered fields that were once closed to them: medicine, business, government, law, and aviation, among others. Congress and the courts forced some changes, in the form of new laws designed to provide equal access to education and employment regardless of race, religion, or gender. The needs of an all-volunteer army brought further changes. As the following brief history shows, changes have been slow, difficult, and controversial.

Ancient to Colonial Times

Throughout history, men have dominated the military, as well as government, religion, and other institutions. Most cultures expected men to protect women and children and to take part in organized military activities. Women assumed major roles in child-rearing and domestic matters, as their cultures deemed appropriate. Biology provides the main rationale for these roles. On average, men are larger, more muscular, and physically stronger than women, which makes them more suitable for activities that require feats of strength. Women can get pregnant and bear and nurse children; at least for infants and very young children, women must be available to provide such care.

Despite tradition and stereotypes, women around the world have pursued martial roles. For example, they have been soldiers, pirates, military planners, cavalry members, and marauders. Ancient tombs, artifacts, drawings, and historical writings from around the world show women as warriors. During the thirteenth century B.C., Ramses II of Egypt encountered a female cavalry in northern Africa. Greek historians wrote of finding organized women soldiers in Africa during the sixth century B.C. Around 332 B.C., "Black Queen Candace of Nubia" faced Alexander the Great atop a war elephant. When Portuguese explorer Duarte Barbosa reached the African coast in 1563, he wrote that, among the king of Benamatapa's troops, "those most renowned for bravery are the female legions, greatly valued by the Emperor, being the sinews of his military strength."[2]

Middle Eastern "battle queens" encouraged troops and sometimes became combatants. During the eighth century B.C., Samsi, a warrior queen in what is now Iraq, fought the powerful Assyrian army. In the third century B.C., Queen Septimia Bat Zabbai was renowned as a warrior and an intellectual who spoke five languages. Under her leadership, Palmyran troops gained control of Egypt, Syria, and other lands. Women in the Middle East also helped to defend their cities during the Crusades.

Other female warriors lived in Asia. Between A.D. 246 and 248, 21-year-old Trieu Thi Trinh led a Vietnamese rebellion against oppressive Chinese rulers, commanding about 1,000 mixed-gender troops in 30 battles. She is recorded as having said, "I will not resign myself to the lot of women, who bow their heads and become concubines. I wish to ride the tempest, tame the waves, kill the sharks. I have no desire to take abuse."[3] Japanese women learned martial arts, and some impersonated men to become samurai. In India, noblewomen learned weaponry, fencing, martial arts, and self-defense, and joined male warriors in battle or fought in all-female units. During the seventeenth and eighteenth centuries, some Indian women led troops against British invaders. During the 1400s, China's Hua Mu-Lan fought for 10 years in more than 100 battles while dressed as a man. She inspired the 1998 Disney animated film *Mulan*. Hsi Kai Ching amassed a fortune while leading a pirate fleet of perhaps 2,000 ships during the early 1800s.

In Europe, Celtic women warriors were known for their vigor and skill with swords and axes. Around 100 B.C., the Roman general Ammianus Marcellinus described them in battle: "neck veins swollen with rage, swinging their robust and snow-white arms, using their feet and their fists and landing blows that seem triggered off by a catapult."[4] During that century, Boadicea, queen of the Iceni, fought the Romans who invaded her kingdom in present-day England. An estimated 100,000 Roman troops died when her troops attacked them in what are now London and Colchester. Historians of that era wrote that Boadicea's troops were mostly women.

Jeanne d'Arc (Joan of Arc) is perhaps the best-known female warrior in western history. In 1429, 18-year-old Jeanne led French soldiers against English troops who controlled parts of France in order to restore Charles, son of the former king, to the throne. After fighting at Orléans and Patay, she led troops into Reims, where Charles was crowned. Members of the French clergy arrested Jeanne for wearing men's clothing and for claiming that her orders came directly from God. They delivered her to the British, who executed her in 1431.

During and after the Middle Ages, European women impersonated men to become knights and soldiers. They also took to the sea. Pirate Grace O'Malley, called "Queen of the West," raided ships between Ireland and Spain during the 1500s. At age 60, she fought at swordpoint against Spanish sailors. During the English civil war of the 1650s, women disguised as men fought with Calvinist and Royalist regiments. Some, like Scotswoman Anne Dymoke, were invited to continue after their identities were discovered. Women's bodies were found among dead British troops after the Battle of Waterloo (1815). One of them, Mary Dixon, had fought for 16 years.

European explorers encountered female soldiers in Latin America, as well. Christopher Columbus mentioned them in his letters, and Pizarro's troops fought women as they battled the Incas. Women also fought with men to oust Spanish rulers during the late 1700s.

Despite these examples, women in military roles were the exception. By the Middle Ages, religious dogma, social conventions, marriage laws, and the tradition of chivalry in Europe dictated that men protect women, who were regarded as the "weaker sex."

Colonial Era to the 1940s

Europeans took these attitudes and traditions with them as they colonized other lands, including the Americas. During the American Revolution (1775–1783), men joined militias while women were assigned roles that supported the troops—as cooks, nurses, laundresses, seamstresses, and messengers. Some women volunteered to be scouts, spies, or couriers, and others joined the army disguised as men. Their motives included patriotism, a longing for adventure, and the desire to accompany loved ones serving in the army.

American colonial leaders at the Second Continental Congress hired the first official women employees in 1775, when they created a hospital department for the army. The hospital could hire civilian nurses. From then on, nursing was an accepted role for women in the military.

During the American Civil War, women again worked in military hospitals and accompanied troops as cooks and laundresses. Others became military scouts, drivers, guides, blacksmiths, gunrunners, spies, and saboteurs. Four hundred women are known to have impersonated men to fight in the Union and Confederate armies. As "Franklin Thompson," 21-year-old Sarah Emma Edmonds served with the Michigan infantry as a soldier, "male" nurse, dispatch rider, and spy. Edmonds later received a veteran's pension—a first for women. After the war, she said, "Patriotism was the true secret of my success."[5] Kate Brownell fought with the 5th Rhode Island Regiment at Bull

Run, among other battles. Her commander called her "one of the quickest and most accurate marksmen in the regiment."[6] Loreta Velasquez, alias "H.T. Buford," fought for the Confederate Army and survived its defeat at Fort Donelson in 1862.

Women continued to care for the sick and wounded. Although the military banned women physicians, some served independently. Dr. Mary Walker received the Medal of Honor in 1861 for treating soldiers under fire at Bull Run—she was the first and only woman to receive this medal. Clara Barton volunteered to take supplies to Union troops and then began to nurse the wounded near combat areas and organized nurses near the battlefields. After the war, Barton founded and directed the American Red Cross.

During the Spanish-American War (1898), Red Cross nurses aided wounded soldiers and the thousands who caught influenza. The Army Nurse Corps (ANC) was created in 1901, followed by the Navy Nurse Corps (NNC) in 1908. At that time, virtually all nurses were women. Women physicians were still banned from the military, however, which tended to downplay women's involvement. The U.S. Army issued this statement in 1916:

> No official record has been found in the War Department showing specifically that any woman was ever enlisted in the military service of the United States as a member of any organization of the Regular or Volunteer Army. It is possible, however, that there may have been a few instances of women having served as soldiers for a short time without their sex having been detected, but no record of such cases is known to exist in the official files.[7]

During World War I, women assumed new roles. Civilian women were working as secretaries, clerks, and telephone operators, and it was suggested that they fill those jobs in the military to free more men for combat. Predicting a manpower shortage, Secretary of the Navy Josephus Daniels directed that women be recruited into the Navy Reserve as "Yeomen (F)," to designate them as female. In 1917, the Marine Corps began to enlist women. About 13,000 women, called "Yeomanettes" and "Marinettes," served during the war. The Army did not form a women's corps, but it did hire female telephone operators to work in Europe as civilian contract employees for the Signal Corps. Military nurses served near combat zones, and some died from enemy fire. Three American nurses who served at a field hospital in France received the Distinguished Service Cross.

The American suffragist movement, which advocated women's right to vote, had been supporting women's causes, including broader roles in the military. Some said that women should perform the same jobs as men, including flying military aircraft. Polls showed that most Americans considered these roles unsuitable for women, however. This debate cooled after the war's end in 1918, but women in every state got the vote in 1920, when the Nineteenth Amendment became law. In 1920, Secretary of War Newton D. Baker appointed Anita Phipps, the daughter of an army family, to the position of director of women's relations, U.S. Army. During her decade-long tenure, Phipps advocated a permanent place for women, with military status. The Hughes

THE LETTER OF THE LAW

The Nineteenth Amendment

The Nineteenth Amendment to the U.S. Constitution, ratified August 18, 1920, states:

Section 1. The right of the citizens of the United States to vote shall not be denied or abridged by the United States or by any State on account of sex.

Section 2. Congress shall have power to enforce this article by appropriate legislation.

Report, issued to the Department of Defense in 1928, recommended that women receive "the same rights, privileges, and benefits as militarized men,"[8] yet no permanent women's corps was formed during peacetime.

Expanding Wartime Roles

As World War II began in 1939, women in war-torn countries joined civil defense units, military organizations, and resistance groups. Although the United States had not yet entered the war, American women involved in health care, aviation, and civil defense prepared to serve. Gender biases persisted, however: In a 1939 Army staff study that discussed the possibility of war, one male officer predicted that "women's probable jobs would include those of hostess, librarians, canteen clerks, cooks and waitresses, chauffeurs, messengers, and strolling minstrels."[9]

In May 1941, Congresswoman Edith Nourse Rogers (R-Mass.) introduced a bill to establish a women's army corps with full military status. Rogers noted the problems female contract workers had faced in World War I, including a lack of legal protection, medical care, or veterans' benefits. Rogers had joined the Women's Overseas Service League and then served as presidential inspector of military and veterans' hospitals. She resolved that "women would not again serve with the Army without the protection the men got."[10]

Bitter debates followed. Many officials opposed the bill. Critics called women in uniform an "insult" to men, and a Southern Congressman said, "Take the women into the armed services, who will then do the cooking, the washing, the mending, the humble, homey tasks to which every woman has devoted herself? Think of the humiliation. What has become of the manhood of America?"[11] Other opponents said that women would displace male civil service workers, and still others opposed militarizing a women's corps.

Some groups, though, supported some integration of women into the armed services. The Army Air Corps (the precursor of the Air Force), which needed to staff its 24-hour Aircraft Warning Service program, and Army Chief of Staff General George Marshall, who foresaw severe manpower shortages, thought that women could be useful. Marshall said that the military should not train men for clerical jobs when qualified women were available. He declared, "There are innumerable duties now being performed by soldiers that can actually be done better by women."[12] First Lady Eleanor Roosevelt urged that women be organized in all the service branches.

Congresswoman Rogers's bill gained ground after the Japanese bombed the U.S. naval base at Pearl Harbor, Hawaii, on December 7, 1941, bringing America directly into the war. Congress approved a modified bill, and, on May 14, 1942, President Franklin D. Roosevelt signed Public Law 77-554, creating the Women's Auxiliary Army Corps (WAAC). The corps had auxiliary, not full military, status. The Army would provide uniforms, housing, food, health care, and salaries—although these were lower than the Army paid men with similar duties. Women could serve overseas but without the usual overseas pay, government life insurance, veteran's medical coverage, and death benefits. WAACs could not command men.

Critics objected to "women soldiers" and decried the fact that married women could become WAACs without their husbands' permission. Religious groups suggested that the WAAC was part of a plot to remove women from traditional domestic roles. Oveta Culp Hobby, a lawyer, journalist, and wife of a former governor, was appointed as a major and head of the WAAC. Major Hobby told critics, "The gaps our women will fill are in those noncombatant jobs where women's hands and women's hearts fit naturally. WAACs will do the same type of work which women do in civilian life."[13]

During the war, more than 150,000 women joined the WAAC (later WAC). Initially, most worked as typists, stenographers, drivers, or with Aircraft Warning Service units. More

This poster is typical of the recruitment efforts of the Women's Army Corps (WAC) during World War II. WACs held a variety of jobs considered appropriate for women, in areas such as cryptology, telegraph operation, and photograph analysis.

than 1,200 WACs in the Signal Corps were telephone, radio, or telegraph operators; cryptologists; or photograph or map analysts. Later, women filled other roles. For example, WACs in the Army Air Forces (AAF) were weather forecasters, cryptographers, radio operators and repairmen, sheet metal workers, parachute riggers, aerial photograph analysts, and control tower operators. By January 1945, only half of them held traditional clerical jobs. Some performed flying duties; one woman aviator died when an aerial broadcasting plane crashed.

Abroad, WACs operated communications systems, plotted troop movements, and organized supply deliveries. Of the WACs who served throughout his campaigns in North Africa, the Mediterranean, and Europe, Lieutenant General Dwight D. Eisenhower later wrote, "[they] have met every test and task assigned them . . . their contribution in efficiency, skill, spirit and determination is immeasurable."[14]

Early in 1943, negative publicity plagued female soldiers. Critics questioned their morality and claimed that the WAACs had high rates of pregnancy and sexually transmitted diseases. One journalist claimed that the Army issued condoms to WAACs—a lie that he had to retract. Investigators found that some of the soldiers who spread these rumors had never met a WAAC. Major Hobby provided statistics that showed extremely low rates of pregnancy and sexually transmitted diseases among WAACs, but these kinds of accusations and character attacks continued through the years as women pursued careers in the traditionally all-male military. In July 1943, however, Congress authorized converting the WAAC into the regular Army as the Women's Army Corps (WAC). This gave WACs salaries, benefits, and titles that were commensurate with men's.

After Congress authorized women in other services in 1942, about 100,000 women became Navy WAVES (Women Accepted for Voluntary Emergency Service) and more than 23,000 joined the Marine Corps Women's Reserve. Marine Corps Commandant General Thomas Holcomb had opposed women Marines but later said, "There's hardly any work at our marine stations that women can't do as well as men. Some work they do far better than men. What is more, they're real marines."[15] Another 11,000 women were Coast Guard SPARS (from the slogan *Semper Paratis*—"Always Ready").

Early in 1942, the Women's Airforce Service Pilots (WASP) was formed. Directed by Jacqueline Cochran, these 2,000 women flew the B-29 Superfortress, YP-59, P-51 Mustang fighter, and other military aircraft, clocking more than 60 million miles in the United States, Canada, and Europe. They moved planes where they were needed and tested new aircraft, freeing men for more combat missions. Some flights were dangerous, and 38 WASPS died on duty. In 1944, Army Air Forces Commander General Henry "Hap" Arnold addressed the WASPs, saying,

> The entire operation has been a success. It is on the record that women can fly as well as men. Certainly we haven't been able to build an airplane you can't handle. From AT-6s to B-29s, you have flown them around like veterans. One of the WASPs has even test-flown our new jet plane.[16]

Nurses who served during the war—57,000 in the Army Nurse Corps and 11,000 in the Navy Nurse Corps—often endured rough conditions. Many faced enemy fire while working in mobile hospital units, as flight nurses evacuating wounded men, in France after D-Day, and in other settings. Eighty-three nurses became Japanese prisoners of war.

On the home front, women worked in defense plants and in other jobs traditionally done by men. "Rosie the Riveter" became the symbol for all women dressed in protective gear operating power tools and building ships, aircraft, and other military equipment.

After the war, women in the armed services received numerous medals, citations, and commendations for courage and dedication to duty, including posthumous awards for those

**The classic image of "Rosie the Riveter" (above) was intro-
duced during World War II to encourage woman on the
home front to take up jobs traditionally held by men. The
inspiration for Rosie was Rose Will Monroe, who worked as
a riveter building military airplanes.**

killed by enemy fire. By December 1946, though, WACs num-
bered less than 10,000, working mostly in office jobs, and only
a few hundred women Marines remained on duty. The WAVES,

WASP, and SPARS programs were dismantled. Women defense plant workers were dismissed. Most Americans of both genders agreed that women should resume their traditional roles now that the crisis was over. Men continued to be drafted for service whereas women's service was voluntary and limited.

A Permanent Place

Women's performance during the war did lead Congress to consider giving them a permanent, though limited, role. After two years of debate, Congress passed the Women's Armed Services Act of 1948 (206-133). It established the Women's Army Corps and authorized women in the Army, Navy, and Air Force and their reserve components. Conservative lawmakers demanded certain limits: Women could make up no more than 2 percent of the armed forces, and caps were set on the number of female officers permitted and the ranks women could attain. They could not command men or serve in ground combat or on naval ships, except hospital ships and certain transports. They were denied spousal benefits unless their husbands relied on them for more than half of their support. Executive Order 10240 (1951) stated that women who were pregnant or became mothers through marriage or adoption could not serve.

By 1950, nine components of the armed forces accepted women: the Army Nurse Corps, Navy Nurse Corps, Air Force Nurse Corps, Air Force Medical Specialists Corps, Army Medical Specialists Corps, Women's Army Corps, Women's Air Force, Women's Naval Reserve, and Women Marines. In 1951, Secretary of Defense George Marshall urged that the Defense Advisory Committee on Women in the Services (DACOWITS) be formed, in order to report to the Department of Defense about matters concerning women in the military and to improve the recruitment of women.

Between 1952 and 1955, however, the number of women in the military fell from 48,700 to 35,000.[17] During these peacetime years, recruitment was not a priority. Also, women were banned from certain Military Occupational Specialties (MOSs). This restricted their career tracks, whereas civilian women were enjoying more career options. To attract top candidates, service branches raised their requirements and improved women's opportunities. In 1967, Congress took a major step by striking down the 2 percent quota for women and the limits on their ranks and pay grades. The Armed Services Committee was quick to say, however:

> There cannot be complete equality for men and women in the matter of military careers. The stern demands of combat, sea duty, and other types of assignments directly related to combat are not placed upon women in our society . . . . a male officer in arriving at the point where he may be considered for general and flag rank passes through a crucible to which the woman officer is not subjected—such as combat, long hours at sea, and other dangers and isolations.[18]

During the 1960s, U.S. military involvement in Vietnam escalated and antiwar protests accompanied rising casualty rates. As more men sought deferments, women were recruited for non-combatant jobs. When U.S. troops withdrew from Vietnam in 1973, more than 6,000 nurses had served in hospitals, evacuation units, flight crews, and Mobile Army Surgical Hospitals (MASH). Modern weapons and guerilla warfare caused grave injuries, and nurses sometimes treated more than 100 soldiers per hour. Some nurses were killed; others suffered physical and emotional trauma, as did thousands of veterans, who did not receive the respect or gratitude accorded to veterans of prior conflicts.

The military worked to improve its image and attract recruits of both genders. Feminists and others pushed for change. In 1969, women were first admitted to the Air Force ROTC and the Joint Armed Services Staff College. The Coast Guard opened its regular forces to women. Women also reached new ranks: Two female Army generals received their stars in 1970. The next year, the Air Force promoted two women to brigadier generals and the Navy named its first female rear admiral. In 1974, the Marine Corps named its first female brigadier general. Mary Clarke became the Army's first female major general in 1978.

The Volunteer Military

More jobs opened up for women after the nation adopted an all-volunteer military in 1973 and recruiters actively sought more women. The proportion of women serving in the Navy grew from 2 percent in 1945 to 5 percent in the late 1970s and 11 percent by the 1990s. Surveys showed that women joined the military for reasons similar to men's: economic benefits, job security, education, a career path, independence, patriotism, and chances to travel and meet new people.

The 1970s saw many firsts, often prompted by new laws as well as the efforts of DACOWITS. Women challenged policies that automatically discharged mothers and stepmothers and denied their husbands the benefits that servicemen's wives received. After a federal judge struck down the law banning women from all naval ships, the Navy opened noncombatant ships to women in 1978. Women were permitted on all Coast Guard ships, which are entirely noncombatant, and 1977 saw the first mixed-gender crews on two Coast Guard cutters. The 1948 law still banned women from flying combat planes, firing missiles and artillery, and serving on combat ships, but the Air Force opened flight training to women in 1973. Lieutenant Sally Murphy became the Army's first female helicopter pilot. Roles for women pilots soon became a major topic of debate, because the women were assigned to positions that did not involve combat regardless of their performance or class ranking.

Impassioned debates preceded Congress's decision that the military service academies would admit women starting in 1976. In 1979, the women's corps became part of the regular military and the names WAC, WAVES, and SPARS were dropped. Members of the WASP and female Signal Corps operators from

World War I finally received veteran status. An advisory panel made up of women veterans also was formed to suggest policies and programs designed for women. Congress passed a bill in 1983 to provide equal veterans' benefits regardless of age, gender, or race.

By 1980, about 173,450 women were serving in the military and the military had integrated officer promotion lists for men and women. Women could apply for Army jobs in more than 300 of the 345 job categories, including infantry, armor, cannon field artillery, low-altitude air defense artillery, and combat engineering. President Ronald Reagan (1981–1989) announced plans to enlarge the military by 10 percent (approximately 200,000 people), but the Army and Air Force said that they planned to keep the number of women constant. In July 1981, the Military Manpower Task Force, chaired by Secretary of Defense Caspar Weinberger, directed the services to abolish barriers and policies that kept them from maximizing women's abilities. The next year, however, the Army closed 23 MOSs to women, making a total of 61 off-limits. The Army had examined the upper-body strength required for these jobs and rated each

Equal Rights Amendment

The Equal Rights Amendment (ERA), first proposed by suffragist Alice Paul in 1921, was passed by Congress in 1972. Thirty-five states ratified the ERA by the July 1982 deadline—three states short of the total needed for the amendment to become part of the U.S. Constitution. It states, in part:

Section 1. Equality of rights under the law shall not be denied or abridged by the United States or by any state on account of sex.

Section 2. The Congress shall have the power to enforce, by appropriate legislation, the provisions of this article.

MOS according to the probability (called "P factor") of ending up in a combat zone. Under these criteria, women were banned from certain fields in chemical, nuclear, and biological warfare and in logistics. In order to broaden and clarify women's roles in the military, in 1988, the Department of Defense (DoD) issued its "Risk Rule," which required service branches to use a standard approach for deciding which jobs women could fill, with standards based on the likelihood of facing direct combat, hostile fire, or capture.

The 1980s saw gender-integrated military units in action and illuminated women's changing roles. During the 1983 invasion of Grenada, women served as military police, signal and communications officers, helicopter crew chiefs, maintenance personnel, and ordnance specialists. About 1,200 women participated when the Army invaded Panama in December 1989 to remove Manuel Noriega from power. Two women commanded companies. Officially, women soldiers were not in combat positions, but many encountered enemy fire, including Linda Bray and the 15 women in her company.

Big Changes in the 1990s

After the Panama invasion, women were appointed to new leadership roles. In 1990, Captain Marsha Evans became the first woman to command a naval station, Commander Rosemary Mariner became the first woman to command an aviation squadron, and Commander Darlene Waskra became the first woman to command a U.S. naval ship.

Debates over women's roles intensified when about 40,000 women served in the Persian Gulf War. During those six weeks in 1991, women encountered combat situations and found themselves behind enemy lines. Again, some women commanded men. They flew jets and Chinook helicopters, refueled tanks, directed artillery fire, and launched Patriot missiles at Iraqi SCUDs. Two women were captured and later released; 15 were killed. The Marine Corps awarded its Combat Action Ribbon, which signifies engagement with the enemy, to 23 women. The media showed images of women serving in jobs that were once all male and interviewed commanders and government officials who praised their work. Polls showed that most Americans favored expanding women's roles in the military.

The 1992 Presidential Commission on the Assignment of Women in the Armed Forces was set up to study that possibility. In the end, it recommended expanding women's roles in every branch as long as recruits met the standards for the job. The commission opposed assigning women to direct ground or aircraft combat positions but said that women should serve on combatant ships other than submarines and amphibious vessels. That year, women made up 11.4 percent of the active duty forces and 13.3 percent of the reserves (totaling 2,002,600 and 1,127,600 people respectively).

More barriers fell under President Bill Clinton (1993–2001). On April 28, 1993, Secretary of Defense Les Aspin ordered the services to drop most restrictions on women in aerial and naval combat, making them eligible to fly aircraft in combat and serve on warships. Aspin told the services that they must justify excluding women from any job. In response, the Marine Corps said that women could apply for positions as aircraft pilots and crew members and take on more ground combat jobs with a low chance of combat engagement. The Navy allowed women to apply for service on combatant ships. In 1994, Aspin repealed the Risk Rule and instituted the new Direct Combat Probability Code, which measures risks in terms of unit more than geography. Certain restrictions have remained to keep women out of direct ground combat, submarines, and support units that are collocated with direct ground combat forces.

The military was more gender integrated than ever before as it faced new tests in the twenty-first century. U.S. troops were deployed to Afghanistan in 2001 and then Iraq in 2003. By mid-2006, tens of thousands of women had served in the Middle East. The Pentagon reported that 60 female troops had been killed and 370 wounded in Iraq. By then, the United States had the highest concentration of female soldiers on active duty in the world. About 362,000 women were on active duty or in the National Guard or reserves, making up 15 percent of the total active forces (19 percent of the air force, 15 percent of the Army, 15 percent of the Navy, and 6 percent of the Marine Corps) and 25 percent of the reserves. The United States also had the highest number of women in senior ranks, including four with the three-star equivalent rank of lieutenant general or vice admiral, and 2 million female veterans.

Summary

Women continue to make history as they operate on land, in the air, and at sea. Both men and women, military and civilian, offer opinions about how, when, and where women should serve in light of the military's mission: to protect and defend the interests of the United States and its allies at home and abroad. These opinions reflect various political, cultural, social, and religious beliefs, as well as ideas about military effectiveness. The following chapters explore arguments on both sides of some ongoing debates.

Restrictions Against Women in Combat Should Remain in Place

On June 23, 2005, 3 female Marines were killed and 11 more seriously injured when a suicide bomber struck their convoy near Fallujah in Iraq. These women were assigned to checkpoints where people enter and leave the city, a risky job that entails searching people for explosives. Each day, they traveled to and from the checkpoints with security trucks, along roads that were often lined with snipers. Intelligence reports had indicated that Iraqi insurgents were planning attacks targeting U.S. military women. As these Marines were returning to base, the bomber drove into their convoy and other insurgents staged an ambush. This deadly attack intensified ongoing debates about women in combat. Observers noted that the women behaved courageously and those who were able returned fire and risked death to save injured comrades. Opponents of women in combat restated their position that women should not be assigned to ground combat missions or to any area where they might encounter enemy fire or be captured. Such assignments violate rules set by Congress and the Department of Defense (DoD). In response to pressure from these critics, Congress agreed to scrutinize policies governing women in combat.

In 1978, the DoD defined "close combat" as "engaging an enemy with individual or crew-served weapons while being exposed to direct enemy fire, a high probability of direct physical contact with the enemy's personnel, and a substantial risk of capture." The Army used that definition to decide which positions women could not fill. In 1982, the Army began to use the term "direct combat," which uses the previous definition for "close combat" with this addition: "Direct combat takes place while closing with the enemy by fire, maneuver, or shock effect, in order to destroy or capture and while repelling assault by fire, close combat or counterattack."[19]

This exclusionary policy should remain in place and should be more strictly enforced. To send women into combat is not good for the military, for women, or for society in general. It

U.S. Army Definition of "Direct Combat"

No federal statutes ban women from serving in ground combat units. Army and Marine Corps policy does exclude women from assignments to units that are likely to become engaged in direct combat, however. The Army defines "direct combat" as follows:

> Engaging an enemy with individual or crew-served weapons while being exposed to direct enemy fire, a high probability of direct physical contact with the enemy's personnel, and a substantial risk of capture. Direct combat takes place while closing with the enemy by fire, maneuver, or shock effect in order to destroy or capture, or while repelling assault by fire, close combat or counterattack.

threatens national security and military readiness and could lead to unnecessary loss of life, primarily because of women's physical build and the special problems that occur when the genders are thrown together in combat conditions.

Women lack the physical abilities and temperament needed for combat.

Nobody can deny the very real physical differences between men and women, which are verified by extensive research. On average, men are significantly larger, heavier, stronger, and faster than women, with a higher percentage of muscle and bone mass.[20] Men can carry heavier loads at greater speeds and for longer periods of time. They also can throw heavy objects, such as hand grenades, farther.[21] According to Mackubin Thomas Owens, only 10 percent of women can meet all of the minimum physical requirements for 75 percent of the jobs in the Army. He wrote, "Women may be able to drive five-ton trucks, but need a man's help if they must change the tires. Women can be assigned to a field artillery unit, but often can't handle the ammunition."[22] On average, women are about five inches shorter than men and weigh less, with less muscle mass and more fat tissue. Women tend to have shorter legs, which means that they typically march slower than men. With about 10 percent less oxygen-carrying hemoglobin in their blood and an aerobic capacity about 70 to 75 percent of a man's, women also have trouble marching more than 32 miles at a time.

Women also have less upper body strength: a typical woman has about 50 to 60 percent of a man's.[23] Fit women can safely carry about 40 percent of their body weight, but men can carry 55 percent of theirs. The average military-age woman weighs 33 pounds less than the average man, so the average weight-lifting disparity is about 44 pounds.[24]

Combat equipment typically includes survival gear, weapons, ammunition, satellite communication devices, batteries, and water. These items weigh can weigh up to 100 pounds or more, and modern body armor weighs about 25 pounds. This poses problems, especially when speed and distance are important. Many women also lack strength to lift heavy items high enough. In field jobs soldiers may need to lift and then maneuver objects. With smaller hands, women may also have trouble handling certain equipment, such as hand guards for their standard M-16 rifles.

At West Point, women are slower than men to finish the "enduro run," which includes running, climbing ropes, and crawling at high speed. Measurements done by the physical education department have shown that female cadets have one-third the upper-body strength of men and two-thirds the leg strength, with about the same amount in the abdomen. Men showed more power and power endurance, leg power and leg-power endurance, dominant hand–grip strength, and nondominant hand–grip strength.[25]

Training does not reverse inborn differences. When men and women of the same age and weight, in average physical condition, undergo the same intensive physical training, the men are still stronger and faster at the end.

Less physical strength means that women in combat face a higher risk of capture and death. Physical limitations can endanger the women and their fellow soldiers. If a woman cannot carry her equipment or do her job, other soldiers have to step in. Problems, including fatalities, can occur when soldiers lack certain physical capabilities for their assignments. In 2003, 18-year-old Private First Class Melissa Castillo died during a training exercise in South Korea while driving a personnel carrier that rolled over. She was not wearing a seatbelt and was seated in an unsafe way. At five feet two inches, Castillo could not see over the dashboard of the vehicle, so she removed the seat back and then sat on top of it. The military accident report stated that drivers of this vehicle must be at least five feet five inches tall in order to see obstacles on the road.[26]

It is misleading to say that today's military jobs rarely require physical strength. This was untrue during the Iraq War with the assault on Baghdad in 2003 and house-to-house fighting in Fallujah. In today's military conflicts, the battle lines are often referred to as "360 degrees." If the military expected future conflicts to be combat-free, they would end combat training programs and disband combat units.

Furthermore, many believe that men are temperamentally better suited for combat than women. They say that women are by nature less aggressive, which makes them less effective as warriors. They argue that thousands of years of human history show that men are naturally more aggressive and find it easier to carry out warrior roles. About 90 percent of all people arrested for violent crimes are male.[27]

Statistics gathered since the 1990s show that a higher percentage of female veterans suffer from post-traumatic stress disorder (PTSD) than men do, and their PTSD seems more severe.[28] After the Persian Gulf War, female veterans were twice as likely as male veterans to seek treatment for PTSD. In the civilian population, more women than men also seek treatment for PTSD. To learn more, researchers from the Veteran Administration's Clinical Neurosciences Division compared male and female brain function. They concluded that male brains are more efficient at producing neurosteroids—chemicals that help people cope with stress. Women tend to deplete serotonin (a substance that fights depression) faster than men and produce it more slowly.[29]

Sending women into combat conflicts with American values.

Sending women into combat goes against the nation's cultural and religious traditions, including Judeo-Christian values. Some Americans strongly object to women in combat on moral grounds; they often find support for their views in religious doctrines. According to the Council on Biblical Manhood and

Womanhood, "The pattern established by God throughout the Bible is that men, not women, bear responsibility to serve in combat if war is necessary."[30] These roles, said the council, reflect clear biological differences between the genders.

Many Americans contend that placing women in warrior roles defeminizes women and degrades them as people. They believe that women should be protected from harm. Addressing Congress in 1992, retired Marine Corps Commandant General Robert H. Burrow expressed these sentiments when he said,

> Combat is . . . killing. And it's done in an environment that is often as difficult as you can possibly imagine. Extremes of climate. Brutality. Death. Dying. It's . . . uncivilized! And women can't do it! Nor should they even be thought of as doing it. The requirements for strength and endurance render them unable to do it. And I may be old-fashioned, but I think the very nature of women disqualifies them from doing it. Women give life. Sustain life. Nurture life. They don't take it.[31]

Direct Combat Probability Coding System (DCPC)

In 1983, the Army instituted its DCPC classification system in order to evaluate every position based on the duties of the Military Occupational Specialty (MOS) or Area of Concentration (AOC), as well as the unit's mission, strategic policies, and location on the battlefield. Each position is then coded on a scale of P1 to P7, based on the probability of engaging in direct combat. P1 represents the highest probability and P7 the lowest. Women are excluded from positions that are coded P1 and may also be banned from entire MOSs or AOCs if the number or grade distribution of positions coded P1 make it impossible for women to progress in that career area.

Similarly, Gulf War veteran Lieutenant Colonel William Bryan said, "I am not prepared to see America's mothers and daughters paraded down the streets of Baghdad and subjected to abuse, when it's not necessary. Now those are my values as an American citizen."[32]

Those who oppose combat restrictions for women say that women have survived combat situations, including being prisoners of war. They claim that the threat of being raped or tortured is not a valid reason to exclude women. Those who support the restrictions point out, however, that putting women into combat amounts to condoning and even inviting violence against women. Elaine Donnelly, director of the nonprofit Center for Military Readiness, asked, "Is that a step forward for civilization, or is it a step backward?"[33]

The media and the military create false impressions about women's performance.

The public has received a distorted view of women's performance in the military, largely because of the media. The media tend to emphasize women's activities because their roles are relatively new and therefore "newsworthy." Stories about women soldiers have been exaggerated and even falsified as advocates for women in combat use isolated examples in attempts to demonstrate that women can do anything that men can do. These advocates include ardent feminists who want to ignore the differences between the sexes and make men and women interchangeable.

When Army Private Jessica Lynch was captured in April 2003 while serving in Iraq, major newspapers featured photos that purported to show her firing at the enemy. Although stories claimed that Lynch was shooting, she was wounded. Later, Lynch explained that she had not been firing her gun; it was jammed. Likewise, people who oppose women in combat say that the press misrepresented the actions of Sergeant Linda Bray in Panama and other women to dramatize their experiences. Women's activities were emphasized during the Gulf War, yet they made up only 6 percent of U.S. troops deployed to the Gulf.

An Air Force military police officer stands guard on the flight line in this 1994 photograph. Although women are still not allowed in "direct combat" positions, they do serve in some high-risk positions.

Heroic men are often ignored. In 2001, former Army officer John Hillen wrote in the *Wall Street Journal*:

> Americans should be exposed to soldiers like Jason Amerine, the wounded Green Beret captain whose exploits in helping to capture Kandahar [a Taliban stronghold in Afghanistan] were dramatically detailed in the *Washington Post*. . . . It's a shame that more Americans now know of Kelly Flinn, the philandering and lying B-52 pilot, than Capt. Amerine. . . . [He] might be uncomfortable with the publicity, but it serves a greater good.[34]

More examples of media bias came in January 2002 after a KC-130 tanker aircraft crashed in the mountains while making a nighttime landing approach to an airbase in Pakistan. The plane was on a routine supply mission and crashed because of technical reasons. This accident made front pages of major newspapers because one crew member, radio operator Marine Sergeant Jeannette Winters, was the first woman to die after U.S. forces entered Afghanistan in 2001. The *Washington Post* article featured the bold-faced subheading: "Female Radio Operator Among 7 Marines Killed." Language in the article implied that this was a combat mission: "It was the deadliest incident yet, for U.S. forces in the war against terrorism being fought in neighboring Afghanistan, and it brought the first death of a female service member in the conflict."[35] Likewise, the *New York Times* put Winters's photo on the front page and seemed to imply that she was in combat on the front lines. An article in *USA Today* said:

> Now, besides TV images of bearded Green Berets trekking across mountains and burly Marines hunching in foxholes, there's the photo of Sgt. Jeannette Winters . . . who died . . . when their Marine cargo plane crashed in Pakistan. Winters, 25, was one of an estimated 6,000 women warriors who have quietly helped rout the Taliban who had ruled Afghanistan, and the al-Qaeda terrorist network there.[36]

In fact, at that time fewer than 100 American troops, all CIA agents and Special Forces, had fought in actual ground combat. About 1,000 combat Marines stationed near Kandahar had not yet engaged in ground combat.[37]

Journalists paid less attention to the male Marines, including pilot Matthew Bancroft, a father of three children who had voluntarily extended his tour of duty to fight terrorism. The other crewmen also volunteered to serve in Afghanistan. Does one member of the crew deserve more attention than the others? Journalist Gerald L. Atkinson said that emphasizing Winters's role reflects "a radical feminist agenda rather than reporting the news in-depth without gender bias."[38] Critics also said that the coverage implied that women's lives were more valuable than men's.

Military officials have also withheld information about women soldiers when it might upset the public. According to author Kate O'Beirne, officials waited a year to reveal that Rhonda Cornum and Jessica Lynch were sexually molested and beaten when they were POWs during the Iraq War.[39] American citizens deserve a full and realistic picture of today's gender-integrated military so that they can develop informed opinions.

The presence of women in combat units would lower unit cohesion and morale.

Adding women to combat units could cause distractions and special problems that arise from mixing the genders. People who state that men and women work together well in other settings are ignoring the fact that combat units are radically different from any organization in civilian life. Cohesion in these units is unique and springs from a strong sense of bonding under extreme conditions as people struggle to survive.

The bonding that produces a strong, effective fighting force is based on cohesion, loyalty, and confidence in one's comrades. In a presidential report, military experts said, "Unit members [must] become totally dependent on each other for the completion of their mission or survival; and group members must meet all standards of performance and behavior in order not to threaten group survival."[40] Mixing the two genders adds romantic and sexual elements that can cause competition, jealousy, and favoritism, which impair cohesion and loyalty. Romantic pairings exclude, rather than include, other group members. During wartime, commanders must assign people to life-threatening jobs. A leader who shows favoritism or protects a lover can cause resentment, erode discipline, and shake confidence in the leadership. The potential hazards are far more serious than those that result when civilian coworkers form romantic attachments. "No unit can afford to have two people in love with another," said Dr. Anna Simons, a professor at the Naval Postgraduate School, who opposes gender-integrated combat units. "Forget the sex—this is about the clouding of judgment. No matter how close the friendship is between men, it still doesn't jeopardize their decisions the way that love does."[41]

The intense forces that draw men and women together cannot be ignored or eradicated by training, education, or military discipline. People are unlikely to view members of the opposite sex in a gender-blind way while living and serving together in close quarters. Despite the military's strict rules regarding fraternization (that is, the military forbids service members from dating across ranks), sexual activity does occur. This is predictable, especially considering that most recruits are under age 30, are involved in life-and-death situations, and may be deployed at sea or in foreign lands for long time periods. The military saw high rates of sexual activity among troops in the Persian Gulf and Iraq wars. In a Roper poll, 64 percent of the Gulf War veterans reported sexual activity between men and women serving together, and most said that these activities lowered their unit's morale.[42] Romantic relationships and sexual liai-

D'Ann Campbell on Women in Combat

In *Women in Combat: The World War II Experience in the United States, Great Britain, Germany and the Soviet Union*, D'Ann Campbell expressed this opinion:

> The question of women in combat has generated a vast literature that draws from law, biology, and psychology, but seldom from history. The restrictions against women in combat that persisted for decades in the United States were not based on experimental research or from a consideration of the effectiveness of women in combat in other armies. The restrictions were primarily political decisions made in response to the public opinion of the day, and the climate of opinion in Congress.

Source: *Journal of Military History*, April 1993, pp. 301–323. Available online at http://members.aol.com/DAnn01/combat.html.

sons not only complicate the lives of combatants, but they also use energy that could be channeled into work.

Even if policies change, many more men than women will qualify for combat duty. Men's morale will suffer because, traditionally, many men were motivated to fight because they were providing defense for women and children. In 1980, a Marine Corps commandant said that women's participation in combat "would be an enormous psychological distraction for the male who wants to think that he's fighting for that woman somewhere behind. . . . It tramples the male ego."[43] Author Lee Bockhorn put it this way:

> The willingness of men to fight and die in wars for women (rather than alongside them) is not a paternalistic expression of women's inferiority, as feminists would have us believe. Rather, it affirms the superiority of the good life which women represent in any decent society—of home and hearth, of children and future generations, of beauty and love.[44]

Including women in combat would impair military effectiveness.

Combat units that include women will suffer higher rates of personnel loss and other problems that hinder performance. Women are less deployable because they are more prone to injuries, such as stress fractures, and other conditions that are more common among women. Statistics have shown that women are four times more likely to report ill, and, at any given time, about twice as many women as men are medically unavailable.[45]

Pregnancy is one major reason for this. About 60 percent of all military personnel are under age 30, and women in this age group tend to have a higher incidence of becoming pregnant. Between 10 and 17 percent of all servicewomen become pregnant during a given year. In 1988, 51 percent of the single Air Force women and 48 percent of the single Navy women stationed in

Iceland were pregnant. While U.S. troops were stationed in Bosnia between December 1995 and July 1996, a woman had to be evacuated for pregnancy about every three days. The General Accounting Office (GAO) found that women soldiers were four times more likely than men to be nondeployable during the Gulf War because of pregnancy and family responsibilities.[46] Ten percent of the 360 women on board the USS *Acadia* had to be evacuated because they became pregnant during the war.[47] High attrition rates impair readiness because combat units depend on the work of all members, and departures have an adverse impact on unit morale and cohesion. To address such problems, in 1997, the Army felt it necessary to give commanders a handbook discussing ways to prevent pregnancies and other injuries and health problems, such as dehydration and fatigue, that are more common among deployed women.[48] The other service branches have also been compelled to address these problems, which costs time, money, and other resources.

With women fighting in ground combat, casualty rates would increase because most women are not physically as able to survive or help others as the average man. Said Elaine Donnelly, "No one's injured son should have to die on the streets of a future Fallujah because the only soldier near enough to carry him to safety was a 5'2", 110 pound female."[49] Because men are usually taught to protect women, they might put themselves in more danger to protect the women in their units. In attempts to prevent women from being captured, hurt, or tortured, commanders might make decisions or act in ways that run counter to optimal military strategy.

Eliminating the combat exclusion policy could lower recruitment numbers, which will also impair readiness. Many women will not enlist if they fear being assigned to combat duty. Army Research Institute (ARI) studies conducted since 1993 found that 85 to 90 percent of enlisted women oppose being assigned to combat roles on the same involuntary basis as men.[50] A 1998 report from the GAO said that only 10 percent of female privates and corporals agreed with the statement "Women should be treated exactly like men and serve in combat arms just like men."[51] Retention would also suffer: A 1993 poll showed that only 14 percent of the women would remain in the service if they were compelled to serve in combat.[52] Women who train for jobs that seem unrelated to combat situations have said that they did not expect to be under fire and were shocked when that occurred in Afghanistan or Iraq. Some said that they would not have joined the military had they known about these risks. National Guard Sergeant Brenda Monroe told the *Sacramento Bee*, "You're not generally told as a female that you will be in that type of situation where you are in harm's way directly. I never dreamed that I would wake up every night and have to run to a bunker and take cover because we were being attacked or under direct fire."[53]

Most likely, fewer men will enlist or stay in the military if they fear that their fellow soldiers are not fully competent. Besides fearing for their own safety, many men find the idea of women in combat distasteful. In the book *The Kinder, Gentler Military*, Stephanie Gutmann offered many examples of experienced and

Affirmative Action?

In 1989, women made up 10.8 percent of the military, and some observers said that they were being promoted based on affirmative action more than on merit. Social scientist Army Captain Richard D. Hooker Jr. wrote:

> As a group, women in the Army have enjoyed greater promotion success than men for almost a decade. Individually, some less-well-qualified candidates have inevitably been selected for promotion and command—an unavoidable price, perhaps, of a necessary and just commitment to the achievement of parity, but one with unpleasant side-effects just the same.

Source: "Affirmative Action and Combat Exclusion: Gender Roles in the U.S. Army," *Parameters*, December 1989, pp. 36–50.

highly qualified military men who have resigned because they lacked confidence in today's "gender-neutral" military.[54]

Other nations realize that women do not belong in combat. In 1996, the United Kingdom set out to fully integrate its military but later decided against this plan. As of April, women were removed from many positions and placed in all-female platoons. Officials declared that their training regime and subsequent duties would be "commensurate with their physical profile."[55] Women in the British armed forces may not drive tanks, serve in the front-line infantry or on submarines, or serve as mine-clearance divers. They cannot join the infantry, Royal Armoured Corps, Royal Marines, or RAF Regiment. People who advocate women in combat often mention the Israeli army, which drafts both women and men. Women, they say, fought with men during the 1948 war for independence. Israeli women are not assigned to ground combat units, however, despite a 1995 court ruling that struck down the ban against women in combat. After studying research on the physical capabilities of men and women, military physicians concluded that women should not serve in front-line infantry positions, artillery units, or tank crews. Combat-related roles are voluntary, and women may not serve on submarines. Certain countries that permit women to serve in combat, such as Canada and Norway, have primarily peacekeeping forces that have not actively fought in wars for decades.

———●———————●———————●———

Summary

Nearly every culture regards combat as an arena for men. The mission of the military is to prevail against the toughest and most ruthless enemies, which means that U.S. combat troops must be strong, well-trained, highly motivated males. A few women might be able to perform as well as men in combat, but military policies and training programs cannot be based on exceptions. For maximum efficiency, armed forces need to train and assign people based on what the majority can do. As author Stephanie Gutmann pointed out, "An effective fighting force depends on a steady supply of known quantities; it needs 'units' made up of interchangeable elements called soldiers."[56]

Equality is an admirable goal, and America prides itself on its egalitarian ideals and civil liberties. The problems that arise with women in ground combat units will further complicate military missions and sacrifice effectiveness in the pursuit of equality, however. People who aim to bring total gender equality to the battlefield ignore the fact that war is not "fair." Policies must be decided on the basis of military readiness, not equal rights. When gender equality conflicts with military readiness, readiness must prevail.

Women Should Be Eligible to Serve in Ground Combat

On June 16, 2005, Sergeant Leigh Ann Hester, a member of the 617th Military Police, received the Silver Star for gallantry in combat. That March, in Iraq, Hester's squad was shadowing a supply convoy when it was ambushed. The squad moved to surround enemy insurgents and prevent their escape. As the fighting went on, Hester used grenades and her rifle to kill three insurgents. The firefight left 27 insurgents dead, 6 wounded, and 1 captured. When the press noted that Hester was the first woman since World War II to receive the Silver Star, she commented, "It really doesn't have anything to do with being a female. It's about the duties I performed that day as a soldier."[57]

Hester and many other women have found themselves under fire and have returned fire. In the air, female pilots have proven their skill and valor in combat missions. As of 2006, however, women were still not officially assigned to direct combat units,

National Guard Sergeant Leigh Ann Hester, 23 years old, stands at attention before receiving the Silver Star at an awards ceremony at Camp Liberty in Baghdad. Hester was the first female soldier since World War II to receive the Silver Star, which is the third-highest medal for valor in the United States.

battalion-level forward support company positions, or missions of infantry, armor, Special Operations Forces, and Marine infantry. These restrictions are discriminatory and impractical. Men should not be automatically eligible for certain positions while women are banned based solely on gender. Polls show that most Americans agree: In 1980, 44 percent of Americans said that women should be eligible for combat roles. That number rose in 1990, when 72 percent of those surveyed in a *New York Times/ CBS News* Poll said that women should be allowed to serve in combat units if they wish. A McCall's magazine telephone survey of 755 women, conducted in February 1990, found even more support: 79 percent.[58] A Gallup poll taken in 2001 showed that a majority of Americans favored giving women the option to serve in combat.[59] These opinions are based on solid information.

Women have demonstrated their abilities as warriors.

History offers many examples of successful women warriors. As historian and martial arts expert David E. Jones pointed out:

> Both [women and men] attacked enemy strongholds, defended castles, laid sieges, and led expeditionary forces. Both built military empires, dueled for honor with sword and pistol, and designed military strategy. Spying, terrorism, banditry, and piracy, assassination, demolitions, aerial combat, guerilla warfare, hand-to-hand combat—all boast expert women practitioners.[60]

A look at the past century shows women fighting bravely and well. During World War II, women risked capture, torture, and execution to complete dangerous missions, including espionage and sabotage. Soviet women served as sharpshooters, submachine gunners, mortarmen, machine gunners, and signalers in all areas, including cavalries, guerilla units, and infantry units, sometimes as commanders. Pilot Lydia Litvak flew combat missions, as did other women in the 588th Air Regiment, which helped defend Stalingrad. Throughout occupied Europe, Jewish women joined uprisings or hid with partisan groups in forests and other places to plan and conduct attacks against the enemy.

African women used bombs, revolvers, and grenades as they fought the French who controlled Algeria during the 1950s. Women made up 5 percent of the guerilla fighters who fought to liberate Kenya from the British.[61] Women combatants fought with Vietnamese guerilla units against the French during the 1950s, and some women commanded militias in their villages.

When civil war ensued after the French left, women fought on both sides. U.S. troops fought with the South against the Communist North (Vietcong). A veteran of three wars, former Chief of Naval Operations Admiral Elmo Zumwalt once said,

> The most vicious, ruthless, cunning enemy I ever had to fight were the Vietcong women, who had the stamina to keep up with their men in the jungles and marshes and who were very capable of suckling their babies by the roadside and then dropping the baby and picking up a rifle and shooting a sailor in the back.[62]

The Americas saw women in action, as well. In the Caribbean, Fidel Castro said that women who fought with his troops during the Cuban Revolution (1956–1959) showed courage as they engaged in "fierce battle with the enemy."[63] Women made up about 30 percent of the Sandinista National Liberation Front's forces in Nicaragua during the 1970s. Commander Tomas Borge said, "Women were in the front line of battle, whether they threw homemade bombs or were in the trenches. They were in the leadership of military units on the firing line during the war."[64] In El Salvador, women guerilla soldiers fought against the military regime in 1980. One woman, who fought in a group with 250 women and 700 men, said, "[we] went into the towns and took control of them. . . . A woman can become a leader the same as a man, and do everything a man can do. We hold the same desire in our hearts. We only want to have justice and liberty."[65]

In recent decades, tens of thousands of American women have gone to war. In 1989, Air Force Colonel Ronald Sconyers wrote:

> Due to the nature of the Panama invasion, women soldiers quickly found themselves in the "front line" of the conflict doing battle with the enemy. In fact, there were not "front lines" during the hostilities. What was considered to be a

relatively secure area one minute would come under sniper or mortar fire the next.[66]

Women were praised for their performance in Bosnia, and Major General William Nash, head of U.S. forces in Bosnia, said that their performance "was indistinguishable from that of their male counterparts."[67]

Since then, women have assumed more diverse roles and faced new challenges in the Persian Gulf, Afghanistan, and Iraq. Women in the 82nd Airborne Division in Afghanistan completed infantry patrols covering 10 to 20 miles a day over rough terrain while carrying up to 75 pounds of equipment. Sergeant Nicola Hall told a reporter, "As MPs, we search people and look for weapons. . . . I never thought we would be walking for hours or be on the front. [The 82nd Airborne soldiers] have been nothing but respectful to us; as long as you walk, carry your own weight and don't whine, you're respected."[68] During and after a suicide bomber's attack on a Marine convoy in Iraq in 2005, women again showed courage and determination. That day, on hearing about the attack, a group of women Marines stationed near Fallujah approached their commander; one woman said, "Sir, we know we've had women killed. We need to replace them. We want to go."[69]

Women are physically capable of serving in combat.

People who oppose women in combat claim that they lack adequate strength. Certainly not everyone can handle the physical demands of combat, but it is wrong to generalize based on gender. Some women have the capabilities, whereas others, including some men, do not. Some women outperform some men and vice versa. Some men outperform other men.

Although the average man is taller and stronger than the average women, individuals vary. In a study of 623 women, 32 percent were able to meet or exceed men's test scores on an Army

Physical Fitness Test.[70] Striking examples of strong women can be found throughout history; for example, famous circus performers of the late 1800s. Billed as "Minerva," Josephine Blatt of New Jersey performed a hip-and-harness lift of 3,564 pounds. At six feet tall, Blatt weighed about 200 pounds. Other women have lifted three times their own weight. Using just one hand, Austrian Katie Sandwina raised her husband above her head. American Jan Suffolk Todd, called "the world's strongest woman" in 2006, could hoist 1,000 pounds in three power lifts. Athletes, bodybuilders, and other strong women are more than capable of performing ground combat jobs.

Today's women are taller than previous generations, and women's overall physical performance is better, coinciding with expanding athletic programs for girls. Thanks in part to Title IX, recent generations of women have had more access to organized sports. In 1980, West Point Cadet Alice Barry scored a perfect 500 on the ROTC Advanced physical fitness test, which aims to measure all-around physical performance. Since then, other women have also achieved this perfect score.

Some women recruits are already physically capable, and others gain strength through training. A DoD study showed that, with additional training, most women recruits become as strong as an average man.[71] At the beginning of one study, 24 percent of the civilian women subjects could qualify for "very heavy" army

THE LETTER OF THE LAW

Title IX

The Title IX legislation applies both to academic and sports programs in public schools. It states, "No person in the U.S. shall, on the basis of sex, be excluded from participation in, or denied the benefits of, or be subjected to discrimination under any educational program or activity receiving federal aid."

jobs. After a six-month program that included weight training, jogging with 75-pound backpacks, and performing squats while bearing 100 pounds on their shoulders, 78 percent of the 41 civilian women could qualify for these very heavy jobs.[72] Studies at West Point Military Academy show that physical training can improve women's cardiopulmonary efficiency, as well. Women cadets improved in that area to a greater degree than men cadets. In other studies, some women defeated men in hand-to-hand combat after they received intensive training.[73]

Women possess certain physical advantages, as well. In *The Natural Superiority of Women*, anthropologist Ashley Montagu cited research that shows that women have stronger immune systems, which can help them cope better with starvation, shock, exposure, illness, and fatigue. Other research shows that women have more acute hearing. Their leg and abdominal strength are similar to men's. Layers of fat give women more buoyancy in water and enable them to withstand cold temperatures better. Women also tend to perspire more efficiently than men because their sweat glands are distributed more evenly.

Size does not make all the difference, and some outstanding soldiers have been relatively small. Audie Murphy, the most decorated American soldier of World War II, stood five feet, five inches tall. Murphy was initially rejected by every service because of his size, and fellow soldiers called him "Baby." Yet Murphy served in combat and earned 24 medals, including the Silver Star, Bronze Star, Legion of Merit, Distinguished Service Cross, and Congressional Medal of Honor.

Size may even be a drawback, especially in small spaces. Upper-body strength can pose problems, because a high center of gravity may hamper balance and motion. What does count, said David E. Jones, are "footwork, balance, speed, experience, knowledge, mental equilibrium, and sensitivity to movement."[74] Smaller people can learn to move effectively and strike vulnerable parts of their opponents' bodies.

In addition, today's missions involve less hand-to-hand combat. Warfare relies more on technology than on brawn, and many twenty-first–century military technologies are gender neutral. Admiral Frank Kelso has said, "Most of the jobs we do in the Navy are not strength-related. There are some, but what we do is use two or three people. . . . So in my thinking, if a female wants to be in a dirty ol' engine room, and she can do it, why should I stand in her way?"[75]

Women can handle the realities of combat, including capture and imprisonment.

Those who oppose combat roles for women say that women are temperamentally unsuited for combat and are naturally less aggressive and more fragile than men. Although statistics show that men commit more violent crimes, nobody has proven the extent to which aggression results from biology versus socialization. Generations of men have learned to regard warrior roles as masculine. They see themselves as more aggressive and "tougher" than women. Nonetheless, women, both civilian and military, have shown that they can be aggressive, tough, domineering, violent, and cruel. Women have committed brutal crimes. During World War II, for example, female Nazi guards tortured and killed prisoners at concentration camps. In Rwanda, Hutu women have joined men in killing Tutsi men, women, and children.

Scientists question traditional ideas about male and female aggressiveness, noting that, among elephants, lions, tigers, and other animals, females are more aggressive than males and hold dominant positions.[76] As for humans, scientist and historian Robert Briffault wrote, "There is not among primitive men and women the disparity in physical power, resourcefulness, enterprise, courage, capacity for endurance, which are observed in civilized societies and are often regarded as organic sexual differences."[77]

Since pioneer days, American women have shown that they can handle physical deprivation and rough living conditions. Military women have lived like male soldiers in various theaters and had to adjust to extreme climates, a lack of bathrooms and showers, and other rugged conditions. Nurses who served in field hospitals in World War II and Vietnam lived with the constant danger of bombings, as well as physical inconveniences. Army nurses who carried their equipment waded onto the beaches of Anzio, Italy, and later in Normandy, France, after D-Day.

Numerous examples show how women can handle the emotional strains of war. During World War II, 1,300 nurses cared for the wounded while bombings continued on the beaches of Dunkirk, France.[78] British women who worked in antiaircraft batteries were praised for their calm efficiency, and a medical examiner said that women "perform the job in hand with calmer deliberation than men."[79] At Anzio, Italy, where six nurses died, First Lieutenant Mary Roberts Wilson was among five nurses who received the Silver Star for evacuating 42 patients and continuing to care for the wounded in surgical tents while under fire. After the war, studies showed that, in London districts with the heaviest bombing, 70 percent more men than women suffered mental breakdowns.[80] In a letter to his superiors that described troop conduct in Vietnam combat zones in 1968, a male Air Force senior master sergeant wrote, "I guess what impressed me most was the calm [with which] the female service members went about their duties (WAF, WAC, WAVES, and Marine). That belief that the frail (or fair) sex will tremble at the first sign of trouble is not true."[81]

Many have suggested that women veterans show higher rates of post-traumatic stress disorder (PTSD) than men, but recent statistics dispute that theory. By 2006, about 137,000 women had served in Afghanistan and Iraq, where many endured surprise attacks, shellings, bombings, and the loss of comrades. Army researchers who studied the impact of war on returning soldiers noted that men and women showed symptoms of PTSD and other mental health problems at about the same rates.[82] Careful screening and selection of recruits can keep out women with a high risk of PTSD. Studies conducted in the 1990s showed that women with a prior history of sexual or childhood abuse are more likely to develop PTSD during their military experience. Moreover, statistics do not tell the whole story; women are more likely than men to seek medical attention, and only those who seek help can be counted in such studies.

Another argument states that women face more dangers, including sexual assault, as prisoners of war (POWs), yet male POWs may also be tortured and assaulted. To prepare for the possibility of capture, female pilots, flight officers in aircrews, and certain other recruits receive training at a SERE (survival, evasion, resistance, escape) school.

Women have survived being POWs. During World War II, 83 Army and Navy nurses were held for three years in the Philippines. Researchers later studied the experiences of 500 survivors of these camps, male and female. Overall, women had less weight loss, less evidence of mental stress, and lower rates of mental breakdown and death from disease or suicide.[83] The nurses, all of whom survived, said that they had tried to stay together as a group, chose leaders to deal with their Japanese captors, and worked as much as possible. The researchers found that they exhibited positive attitudes, discipline, and resourcefulness. In 1944, an American secret agent, parachuter Rolande Colas de La Nouye, was captured by the enemy in France after she helped to gather intelligence for the D-Day invasion. She was tortured and sent to a prison camp until Allied troops liberated the camp at the war's end. De La Nouye continued her work as a secret agent for the West and was made an honorary Green Beret.

During wars in the Persian Gulf and Iraq, women have become POWs. One of them was Major Rhonda Cornum, a physician who volunteered for a rescue mission on February 27, 1991, when the Black Hawk helicopter carrying her team was shot down behind enemy lines. Five of the eight crew members died. Left with a bullet in her right shoulder, two broken arms, and a shattered knee, the 36-year-old Cornum was a prisoner for eight days. She was interrogated and sexually molested. One night, her captors held guns against her head. Now a colonel and graduate of the War College, Cornum has said,

> Every 15 seconds in America, some woman is assaulted. Why are they worried about a woman getting assaulted once every 10 years in a war overseas? . . . . Clearly it's an emotional argument they use (to argue that women should be kept away from the frontlines) because they can't think of a rational one.[84]

Critics have said that Americans cannot tolerate female casualties, but male and female lives have equal value. As soldiers have died in the Persian Gulf, Afghanistan, and Iraq, people do not seem more upset over women's deaths. *NBC News* correspondent Fred Francis, who covered the Pentagon, wrote, "The military totally misread for years how the public would respond to women dying in combat."[85]

Excluding women violates legal principles and implies that women are not full-fledged members of the military.

Fairness and equality demand that women have the opportunity to perform any job if they can meet the requirements. U.S. laws,

THE LETTER OF THE LAW

Fourteenth Amendment

Section. 1. All persons born or naturalized in the United States and subject to the jurisdiction thereof, are citizens of the United States and of the State wherein they reside. No State shall make or enforce any law which shall abridge the privileges or immunities of citizens of the United States; nor shall any State deprive any person of life, liberty, or property, without due process of law; nor deny to any person within its jurisdiction the equal protection of the laws.

including the Fourteenth Amendment and civil rights legislation, ban discrimination based on gender, race, or religion. Dr.
Kenneth L. Karst, a law professor at UCLA, is among those who
argue that segregating women into noncombat positions violates
the Fourteenth Amendment principle of equal national citizenship.[86] This amendment has been applied to cases involving
gender discrimination since 1971. Although cases that involve
gender discrimination have not received the strict judicial scrutiny that is applied when cases involve racial discrimination, they
do receive a fairly high level of scrutiny. In the majority opinion
for *United States v. Virginia et al.*, Justice Ruth Bader Ginsburg
declared that litigants who wish to justify a gender-based law
must present an "exceedingly persuasive" argument.[87]

When military women are excluded from certain roles, they
may be regarded as second-class citizens, as well as less competent and therefore less worthy of respect. This can lead to resentment, especially if men believe that women are receiving special
advantages. Resentment sets the stage for harassment, including
sexual harassment. It can also produce negative economic conse-
quences. When they cannot compete for all jobs, women are less
able to advance and receive certain promotions, which means
that relatively few women can hold top positions.

The way in which the military treats women affects the
larger society. Kenneth Karst pointed out, "When the national
government excludes servicewomen from combat positions,
and purports to exclude gay and lesbian Americans altogether,
those exclusions work grievous material and stigmatic harm to
servicemembers numbering in the hundreds of thousands."[88]
Furthermore, assuming that men alone can be warriors places
special burdens on men and puts women in submissive and
dependent roles. David E. Jones cited the negative impact on
both genders:

> Women who do not understand that they have equal claim on
> this warrior tradition might doubt their places in the subtle

and not so subtle power grid of the modern state society. . . .
Men and women will never reach a common consciousness of
their equality as humans until both accept that women have a
claim on the title "Warrior."[89]

Women are entitled to play an equal role in national defense.
Military personnel take the same oath to protect and defend the
Constitution of the United States against all enemies, foreign
and domestic. They receive equal pay and benefits. Fairness
demands that they assume the same risks and responsibilities
and have access to equal opportunities. Men do not necessarily
want to serve in combat or perform certain other unappealing
jobs either, but both genders realize that they must perform their
duties.

Military efficiency demands that people be assigned on the basis of need, not gender.

Banning women from combat and units that operate in combat
zones can hamper military effectiveness. Military leaders must
be able to assign people as needed with the flexibility to fully
utilize all personnel; the basis for assignments must be competence, not gender. While fighting in Afghanistan and Iraq, the
U.S. military has lacked enough male recruits to staff all of its
ground combat and ground combat support units. Military officials urged the Pentagon to permit mixed-gender forward support companies to collocate with armor and infantry battalions
as a "unit of action."

Furthermore, the lines of combat are unclear and constantly
shifting, because today's wars involve long-distance missiles,
terrorist attacks, and guerrilla fighting. People in so-called "non-
combat positions" are vulnerable. Like infantry soldiers, medics
and supply truck drivers have been under fire, and their vehicles
are less safe than tanks, from which women are banned. Female
soldiers often work in communications centers and supply lines,
however, which can be targets for enemy bombs.

Critics say that women are less deployable than men and that this will cripple combat units. Studies conducted between 1973 and 1993 showed that men as a group had more lost time than women, even when pregnancy was considered.[90] The men lost more time for other reasons, such as alcoholism, drug abuse, disciplinary problems, and going AWOL (away without leave). A study conducted during the 1990s also showed that military women, on average, spent only one hour less per week on the job than men. When maternity leave is excluded, military women had lower rates of lost job time than men.[91]

What about the argument that combat units will not bond well with women present? Even without strong social bonds, soldiers can perform their jobs effectively, based on training and military rules. Discipline and self-control help people stay on task and put aside prejudices and emotions that impede performance. Moreover, mixed-gender units do bond. This has happened in foreign militaries as men and women fought together in Vietnam and El Salvador. Commanders have said that both genders work harder when they fight together because women

THE LETTER OF THE LAW

Civil Rights Act of 1964

SEC. 703. (a) It shall be an unlawful employment practice for an employer—

(1) to fail or refuse to hire or to discharge any individual, or otherwise to discriminate against any individual with respect to his compensation, terms, conditions, or privileges of employment, because of such individual's race, color, religion, sex, or national origin; or

(2) to limit, segregate, or classify his employees in any way which would deprive or tend to deprive any individual of employment opportunities or otherwise adversely affect his status as an employee, because of such individual's race, color, religion, sex, or national origin.

want to prove their competence and men do not want to be out-done.[92] In a combat situation, all members realize that they must cooperate to survive. Colonel Guido Van Oppen commanded a Dutch armored battalion that included both genders. When asked about the impact of women in his unit, he said, "The men basically act normal. It makes no difference whether it's a man or woman . . . act as a soldier, as a professional."[93] Army Captain Cynthia Mosley, who commanded a combat support company in the Persian Gulf, said, "When the action starts every soldier does what they're trained to do. Nobody cares whether you're male or female."[94]

Other nations have lowered barriers against women. Five NATO nations—Canada, Denmark, Luxembourg, Norway, and Portugal—have no combat exclusion laws or policies, and six NATO nations assign women to at least some combat positions. As of 1985, Norwegian women could serve in all

Major Everett S. Hughes on Women in Combat

Major Everett S. Hughes served during World War I. In his 1928 memo to the Assistant Chief of Staff, he offered his insights about the debate over women in combat:

> Some of us conclude that women have no place in the Theater of Operations, others that women have no place in the combat zone. We fail to consider that the next war is never the last one. We forget, for example, that what was the Combat Zone during the World War may be something else during the next war. We use technical terms that are susceptible to individual interpretation, and that change with the art of war, to express the idea that women should not participate here, there, or yonder. We are further handicapped by man-made barriers of custom, prejudice and politics, and fail to appreciate how rapidly and thoroughly these barriers are being demolished.

Source: E.S. Hughes, "Memorandum for the Assistant Chief of Staff, G-1. Subject: Participation of Women in War," September 28, 1928.

combat functions except submarines; in 1995, Norway became the first NATO country to allow women on military submarines.[95] Women may also serve on submarines in Australia, Spain, and Canada. Canadian women have been eligible for all combat positions since 1987, and some have qualified for ground combat positions by meeting the same standards as men. Some women outperform both males and other females. For example, one woman ranked first in parachute training. Denmark opened all units to women in 1988. As of 2006, Danish and Norwegian women were serving in all areas except as para-rangers and marine commandos. They are eligible for these roles, but no woman has met the requirements. Greece, Turkey, and the Netherlands have no laws that ban women from combat.

Summary

As with any military job, combat assignments should be based on individual capability, with no gender automatically included or excluded. As long as performance standards for the job are the same for everyone, competent people should be able to serve in those jobs. Despite claims that combat is "a man's job," women have shown themselves fit for that job. Performing these roles does not make women less feminine or more masculine. It expands ideas about gender roles and can allow both men and women to reach their potential. Traits that soldiers need—courage, strength, aggressiveness, patriotism, and competence—are found in both genders.

Marine Corps Brigadier General Thomas Draude, whose daughter, Loree Draude, distinguished herself as a naval pilot, responded to the question, "Would you let your daughter fly in combat with the possibility of her becoming a POW?" He said, "The answer is yes. I believe we have to send our best. If that means it is my daughter or my son, they should go."[96]

Women who join the military are adults who choose to be there. Individual women are ready and able to serve in combat, even if it makes some people uncomfortable. As Air Force General Jeanne Holm said,

> The military is about going to war and a war is about killing and maybe dying for your country. And as the entire nation learned during Operation Desert Storm, being a man or a woman, or being designated a combatant or a noncombatant, has very little to do with who lives and who dies in modern war. Anyone not willing to accept that fundamental reality of military service should find another line of work.[97]

Gender-integrated Training and Units Offer No Benefits and Impair Military Readiness

During the 1990s, a group of older officers who visited their former base camp found that the once-rigorous obstacle course had been renamed a "confidence course." It had been moved indoors and turned into a series of pipes, monkey bars, ladders, and balance beams.[98] Meanwhile, at Fort Jackson, instead of doing push-ups in unison, recruits were being told to do their best at performing push-ups during a set time period. For morning runs, people were placed in "ability groups." In her book *The Kinder, Gentler Military*, author Stephanie Gutmann described these and other changes that have occurred since the military began its policy of gender integration.

The Army first tried gender-integrated training in 1978, but stopped in 1982 when training personnel said that male recruits were not challenged enough and females were suffering high rates of injuries.[99] The 1992 Presidential Commission on the

Assignment of Women in the Armed Forces expressed similar concerns when it recommended that "entry-level training may be gender-specific as necessary" because of the different physical capabilities of men and women.[100] But pressure from feminists and others led to the revival of gender-integrated basic training (GIBT) in 1995 in all branches except the Marine Corps.

This approach defies common sense, solid research data, and experiences with both kinds of training. Gender integration ignores the very real physical differences between men and women and the problems that occur in mixed-gender settings. As part of the Federal Advisory Committee on Gender-Integrated Training, Senator Nancy Kassebaum Baker (R-Kans) said in 1997, "The present organizational structure in integrating basic training is resulting in less discipline, less unit cohesion, and more distraction from training programs."[101] The Committee voted unanimously to recommend an end to GIBT. In 2001, a group of 16 public policy organizations jointly asked the DoD to end GIBT, which they called "inefficient and problematic."[102] Their letter to Defense Secretary Donald Rumsfeld was signed by the Veterans of Foreign Wars, Independent Women's Forum, Coalitions for America, Concerned Women for America, Center for Military Readiness, and Freedom Alliance. GIBT continues, however, despite serious drawbacks.

Gender-integrated training is less rigorous and gives women preferential treatment.

People close to the training process have noted that the quality of training suffers in mixed-gender groups and that discipline is lower. In 1999, 48 percent of the Army's recruit trainers shared these conclusions with the Congressional Commission on Military Training and Gender-Related Issues.[103] Studies conducted by the Army Research Institute (ARI) between 1993 and 1995 showed no enhanced results in the performance of either men or women in GIBT units.

Few women can keep pace with an average male in training. For example, between 1992 and 1998, records kept at an advanced Army ROTC camp showed that only 2.5 percent of the women cadets could finish the two-mile run as fast as an average male (13.5 minutes). During the push-up test, 4.5 percent of the women met the male average score of 60 push-ups, and top-scoring women scored far below the top men. Only 19 percent of the women met the minimum level of aerobic efficiency that was set for the men. These three tests are regarded as effective predictors of military training performance. Furthermore, ROTC cadets who participate in advanced camps tend to be fitter than average soldiers, so these women's scores would be above average for military women.[104]

The U.S. Military Academy identified 120 physical differences between the genders that must be considered during military training. To deal with these differences, training directors have set less rigorous standards, set separate standards for each gender, or blended these approaches. At West Point, cadets once had to run while carrying heavy weapons, but that exercise, along with others, was dropped.[105] Some trainers tell recruits that they are not competing with each other, only against themselves. These lower standards make training less challenging and less rewarding for men.

Moreover, since the 1990s, policies have enabled weaker recruits to pass or complete a task simply by showing that they are trying or doing their best. Women who cannot perform the same exercise or task as men may be given a "comparable" exercise or task instead. At Fort Leonard Wood in Missouri, when women could not toss a hand grenade far enough to pass the standard test, they were allowed to pass with a lower level of performance.[106] Being unable to throw a grenade far enough in wartime could be deadly to a woman soldier and her comrades.

To reduce the number of injuries, service branches and military academies have implemented a system called "gender norming," which measures a woman's performance against other women rather than against men. Women's scores are weighted to make up for the gaps in performance between males and females. Such approaches give women an unfair advantage and create double standards or at least the appearance of preferential treatment.

The British military reversed its position on gender integration after a disastrous experience. In 1998, they set up a "gender-free" policy for physical tests, meaning that all recruits, male and female, had to meet the same standards. Before this change occurred, women had an accident rate of 467 injuries per 10,000 people. When standards were equalized, the injury rate soared to a record high of 1,113 per 10,000. Injury-related discharge rates for women also rose, from 4.6 percent to 11.1 percent. Men's rates remained stable at about 1.5 percent. After four women died during basic training, the Ministry of Defence called for a study of all training facilities. Physicians concluded that women's injuries occurred mostly because they have less muscle strength, less bone mass, and a shorter stride. Many injuries were stress fractures, especially in the knees, ankles, legs, and feet. After one year, the British returned to a policy that is not gender neutral and the women's injury rate declined by 50 percent. Their "gender-fair" approach trains women separately, with training goals that consider the women's physiques. Lieutenant Colonel Ian Gemmell noted, "This study confirms and quantifies the excess risk for women when they undertake the same arduous training as male recruits, and highlights the conflict between health and safety legislation and equal opportunities legislation."[107]

The U.S. Marine Corps wisely continues to separate the genders for basic training, including having female instructors train female recruits and male instructors train the men. In 1996, the Marines toughened basic training for both genders, adding a week to its 12-week program. At the end, recruits must tackle an arduous 54-hour exercise called the Crucible, which requires them to function and work as teams under stressful conditions. The Crucible and certain other exercises would be unfeasible if they had to accommodate both genders simultaneously. Female

Women Marine recruits wait to fire their rifles during basic training at the Marine Corps Recruit Depot at Parris Island in 1985. The Marine Corps has continued its policy of gender-segregated training even as the other services have integrated their boot camps.

Marine recruits have lower rates of injuries and score higher than other services in tests for the elements that produce cohesion, including group identity and respect for authority.

Separate-gender training reduces distractions and the potential for sexual misconduct.

During training, recruits need to make many adjustments and train rigorously to become disciplined military personnel. Separating the genders lets them focus on their work without the added strains of male–female dynamics. Recruits often worry about how to treat the opposite sex in this uncommon situation. Should they ignore each other? Should they try to be friends? Should they attempt to treat both genders the same? Should the men be at all protective toward the women?

Women who have experienced both kinds of training are able to see the differences. Marine Private Sara Turner went through basic army training in a mixed-gender unit and then joined the Marine Corps, where she attended the women's boot camp at Parris Island. Turner said that, in her army training, there was "more tension between males and females" and "sometimes you'll get unwanted attention, men wanting to talk to you."[108]

Problems related to sexual misconduct are far more likely when men and women, many of them in their late teens and early 20s, experience the forced togetherness of mixed-gender training. The resulting dynamics disrupt concentration, discipline, and other goals for training. Predictably, inappropriate conduct occurs, along with competition, jealousy, suspiciousness, broken relationships, and pregnancies. These pregnancies lead to further problems. According to the testimony delivered to the 1992 Presidential Commission on Women in the Military, pregnancy was the number-one reason that female troops stationed with men during Operation Desert Shield, which preceded the Persian Gulf War, could not be deployed.[109]

To address these problems, the military expends considerable resources on sensitivity training and sex education programs and operates special hotlines for reporting abuses. The time, money, and personnel used for these purposes could be devoted to other military concerns, such as antiterrorism, self-defense, and rescue procedures. New rules include the "no touch, no talk" policy and require that women have a "battle buddy" accompany them in various situations in which they might encounter a male soldier. These measures are intended to prevent harassment and other misconduct, as well as false charges of these offenses.

Separate-gender training enhances morale and cohesion.

A primary goal of basic training is to transform diverse individual recruits into disciplined, group-oriented military personnel. They must become a cohesive military unit with confidence in themselves, each other, and their commanders. Meeting the same training standards is one important way to promote cohesion and camaraderie. With gender norming, however, women do not have to meet the same standards, and anything that smacks of preferential treatment can lower both cohesion and morale. When the U.S. Army Research Institute studied recruits' attitudes toward gender-integrated training, it found that unit cohesion was low overall. It was lowest in all-female companies and highest in all-male companies. Men in mixed-gender companies believed that women were treated "easier than males."[110]

Lower or more relaxed standards can make soldiers fear for their safety. In 1999, a panel that surveyed recruits at U.S. army bases found that 60 percent of men and 74 percent of women either said they "disagreed with" or "were not sure" in response to the statement: "The soldiers in this company have enough skills that I would trust them with my life in combat." In response to the statement, "If we went to war tomorrow, I would feel good about going with this company" 63 percent of the men and 76 percent of the women said that they either "disagreed" or "were not sure."[111]

Morale was higher among Marines at base camp. Female Marines, who are trained separately from men, also said that

THE LETTER OF THE LAW

From the Uniform Code of Military Justice

Article 133—an officer may be charged with conduct "unbecoming an officer."

Article 134—prohibits all disorders and neglects to the prejudice of good order and discipline . . . and all conduct of a nature to bring discredit upon the armed forces.

Fraternization—any personal relationship between an officer and enlisted member that is "unduly familiar and does not respect differences in rank and grade where a senior junior supervisory relationship exists."

A female Air Force trainee glances right while in ranks during morning exercises at Lackland Air Force Base in San Antonio, Texas. One of the arguments for gender-segregated basic training is that it may prove to be less distracting for young men and women.

they appreciate their female drill instructors. In 1997, General Charles Krulak, commandant of the Marine Corps, said:

> I've talked to women down at recruit training and they said in no uncertain terms, "we want to look up to a role model that we can identify with. We want to look up and see the battalion commander is a woman. We want to see the drill instructor that they someday want to be, to be a woman. We'll see enough guys in the next four years or 40." [112]

Despite high costs, gender integration shows no proven benefits.

Retention of trained personnel is economical, and, here again, gender-integrated programs fall short. The Marines, who retain single-gender training, have the best record in terms of meeting recruitment goals, and studies show that morale, recruitment, and retention in the Army, Navy, and Air Force have declined.

Women in GIBT have more stress fractures and other injuries, which add significant costs in terms of medical care and military readiness, in addition to lengthening the time period required to train new recruits. The incidence of stress fractures in the Army ranges from 0.9 to 5.2 percent for men and 3.4 to 21 percent for women. As of 2005, medical costs caused by stress fractures among 2,000 female recruits cost an estimated $1,850,000 annually, with 4,120 lost training days.[113] Higher sick call rates for women affect both costs and retention. A 1999 survey showed that, in addition to gynecological disorders and pregnancy, women also had more psychiatric disorders and stress disorders, which disrupt training.[114]

The cost of adding women to various areas of the military can be high. For example, the military spent $1.3 million to reconfigure spaces aboard the USS *Dwight D. Eisenhower* so that women could serve on that ship with men. Changing housing, clothing, and equipment and keeping enough stock to supply both genders adds extra costs, which seem more unreasonable when women must leave their jobs or cannot be deployed because of injuries, illness, or pregnancy. After a six-month tour, 39 women left the USS *Dwight D. Eisenhower* because they were pregnant.[115] During the Gulf War in 1991, women were three

THE LETTER OF THE LAW

Article 134 of the Uniform Code of Military Justice

Fraternization: Under Article 134 of the Uniform Code of Military Justice, fraternization is prosecutable because it hurts "good order and discipline" or brings discredit to the armed forces.

times less likely to deploy with their units than men, again, usually because of pregnancy. This caused resentment because other people had to do the women's jobs until they were replaced. At times, men perceive that some women become pregnant on purpose to avoid difficult or hazardous assignments—this sort of behavior also lowers morale.

Summary

Opponents to gender integration throughout the military view it as a social experiment (spurred primarily by the feminist movement) that damages the national defense. Often, arguments against gender integration seem to include a longing for the "good old days" when tough drill sergeants could push recruits to the limit, using rough language to "turn boys into men."

They also point out that laws can force changes and leaders can force members of military units to work together, but tolerance is not the same as true acceptance or a real sense of belonging. Such feelings cannot be forced, nor can mutual trust or respect. Morale has suffered in recent decades, and high morale is important for an effective military that can recruit and retain qualified personnel. In *The Kinder, Gentler Military*, Stephanie Gutmann cited a 1998 survey of officers who were planning to leave the Navy. Only 25 percent said that they were leaving for "better opportunities as a civilian"; most said that they were leaving for reasons such as "a change in the culture" and "loss of confidence in leadership." Between 1990 and 2000, the number of Army captains who left voluntarily rose by 58 percent. One of these men wrote, "It's not just about the money. People used to stay in because they felt like warriors, making a difference, with commanders they respected, in units they were proud of. Those feelings don't exist today."[116]

Training and Service Should Be Gender Integrated

Yona Owens was a naval interior communications electrician who wanted to serve aboard an oceangoing survey ship. Like other women, Owens had run up against Section 6015 of Title 10, which gave the secretary of the navy authority to "prescribe the kind of military duty to which such women members may be assigned and the military authority which they may exercise." It further stated that women could not be assigned to sea duty except on hospital ships and certain transports, effectively preventing mixed-gender crews on naval ships. Owens and three other women filed a class action lawsuit, claiming that Section 6015 violated their right to equal protection under the law. The court agreed. In July 1978, a judge ordered the Navy to take steps to end such discrimination and base assignments on individual qualifications. Women were now eligible for sea duty, and soon mixed-gender crews became a reality.

By then, Congress had opened the nation's military service academies to women, creating mixed-gender programs at these formerly all-male institutions. In 1956, Mary Ann Bonalsky, a high school junior from New Jersey, wrote to her congressman to ask why she was not eligible to attend the U.S. Naval Academy at Annapolis. In her letter, Bonalsky wrote, "I have equal rights with the man as far as intelligence is concerned."[117] Other women continued to ask that question until finally, in 1976, those walls came down.

Huge changes have occurred since the 1970s, with the integration of the service branches, military academies, and most basic training programs. The service branches use slightly different approaches to training, based on their needs and missions. In 1976, the air force instituted gender-integrated basic training (GIBT). The Navy began GIBT in 1993, just before the first women were assigned aboard Navy combat vessels. The Army sends recruits to three locations: one for combat occupations, a second for combat-support fields, and a third for those who will serve in combat-service support. The second and third training facilities have been gender integrated since 1994, but the first program is all male. The Marine Corps segregates men and women for basic training.

Gender-integrated training prepares recruits for the gender-integrated military.

Since the 1990s, expanding roles for women have meant that women and men are working together in most military areas. It follows that both should be part of the team from the outset, learning and training together. As commander of the Navy's Great Lakes Training Center, Rear Admiral Kevin P. Green said, "It's absolutely essential that men and women train together from the very beginning. In the process of transforming adolescent civilians to sailors, to prepare them for the fleet environment, I don't want to wait."[118]

Besides promoting teamwork, integrated training shows recruits that the military values both genders equally, which fosters respect among newcomers who arrive with diverse attitudes and backgrounds. Brigadier General Evelyn "Pat" Foote, an officer who has extensive military experience and firsthand experience with GIBT pointed out,

> Gender integrated basic combat training ensures that the training is the same, as well. Gender integrated training, unconstrained by artificial barriers, enhances military readiness and produces soldiers who are highly motivated team members, equally trained and ready to serve the nation as they have sworn to do.[119]

This kind of training leads to effective teamwork on the job. In 2000, for example, after terrorists bombed the USS *Cole*, its mixed-gender crew displayed teamwork and efficiency as they saved their ship, despite massive damage and daunting conditions. These relatively young servicemembers had received gender-integrated training.

GIBT is effective and challenging.

During the 1990s, the 105th and 106th Congresses considered laws that would mandate gender-segregated basic training but ultimately rejected these laws after they examined the evidence, including studies of training programs in the service branches. For example, a 1992 study by the Defense Equal Opportunity

FROM THE BENCH

Owens v. Brown

In *Owens v. Brown* (1978), Judge Sirica ruled that the 1948 statute was unconstitutional. Section 6015's ban on assigning women to ships "was premised on the notion that duty at sea is part of an essentially masculine tradition ... more related to the traditional ways of thinking about women than to military preparedness."

Management Institute (DEOMI) conducted for the Navy found that GIBT units yielded the same performance results as segregated units but with higher levels of teamwork.[120]

Other studies have not shown a negative impact on performance. One study, conducted in 1993 at Fort Jackson, South Carolina, looked at the performance of all-male companies, all-female companies, and mixed companies—50 percent of each gender and 75 percent men/25 percent women. Training officials examined the scores attained for physical fitness and basic rifle marksmanship skills. Scores for men and women in the mixed-gender groups were as good as or better than those attained by members of single-gender companies.[121]

A 1996 study by the ARI recorded scores from physical fitness, marksmanship, and individual proficiency tests over a three-year period. Female trainees in GIBT units performed better, and the men's performance was about the same. The GAO then compared these results with results from all-male basic training companies from 1993 to 1995. Men in gender-integrated companies had higher pass rates than men in all-male companies in the Army Physical Fitness Test and basic rifle marksmanship test.

At the request of Congress, the GAO examined the performance of men and women in GIBT. In its 1996 report, the GAO concluded that the available data from the Army and Navy show that GIBT programs are effective. No data were available from the Air Force. In July 1999, the Congressional Commission on Military Training and Gender-Issues issued a report that stated that gender-integrated training was effective and that there was a side-benefit: Retention rates for women had risen since GIBT began in 1995, with 2 to 5 percent more women completing basic training.

Opponents of GIBT claim that the programs are "watered down" and less challenging than programs designed just for men. The evidence says otherwise. For example, drill sergeants at Fort Leonard Wood said that they have noticed men working harder in basic training, as males try to look good in front of female recruits and as women try to demonstrate their compe-

Men and women at Air Force Basic Military Training School perform a physical training run. Those who support gender-integrated training say that it better prepares recruits for the gender-integrated military.

tence. Male and female trainees were achieving similar scores on basic rifle marksmanship with the M-16, and drill sergeants noted higher passing rates for both genders after training became gender integrated.[122]

The gap between physical fitness test standards for men and women has been closing in recent years. Because of greater participation by girls in sports in elementary and high schools, the gap is expected to close even further. Today's female recruits enter with higher levels of physical fitness than they did in the 1970s. At one time, women in basic training in the Marine Corps would run 1.5 miles to the men's 3 miles. Now, both women and men run 3 miles, with women permitted to run at a somewhat slower rate. Starting in 1998, both genders in the Marine Corps were expected to do 80 sit-ups in two minutes; previously, women were required to do only 50 sit-ups in this time period.[123] Women have problems with larger, more awkward weapons such as the shoulder-held AT-4 anti-tank weapon, but this is also true for men who are smaller and shorter than average.[124]

Adjustments can be made to help both genders reach their potential. People with greater physical abilities can be challenged to go beyond minimum requirements. Standards can be gender normed to minimize injuries and enable women to succeed at levels that take their physical differences into account. The Army also has found that better equipment and sports medicine techniques help recruits reach their potential. The use of athletic shoes rather than boots and other changes have reduced the incidence of injuries. Research goes on to show more ways to prevent and treat stress fractures, which occur more often among women recruits.

Many critics of GIBT focus on physical performance and ignore other aspects of training in which women do as well as, or better than, men. Studies have shown that female recruits tend to be better educated, score higher in aptitude tests, and have fewer discipline problems during basic training.

Mixed-gender military groups can be cohesive and effective.

Experts who study cohesion in the military identify trust, respect for one another's skills, and a feeling of being "like a family" as vital ingredients. These qualities can develop in mixed-gender groups. During World War II, for instance, women in Britain worked in antiaircraft batteries with men. Studies showed that mixed-gender batteries performed even better than all-male groups.[125]

Leadership is crucial in promoting efficiency and appropriate behavior. Brigadier General Evelyn "Pat" Foote commanded a gender-integrated battalion. She later said,

> First, I learned that male and female recruits will obey their leaders and do what they are told to do. When leaders establish clear standards of performance and conduct, set the example, and enforce the standards decisively, taking quick action to deal with violators, then, recruits respond correctly.

Regarding morale and cohesion, Foote said:

> By integrating men and women within platoons down to the squad level, these soldiers learned the value of teamwork early and learned to appreciate the skills each soldier contributed to the successful accomplishment of group tasks. A natural byproduct of the pride soldiers feel when they get the job done is mutual respect of one another regardless of gender. Cohesive squads are the essential building blocks of cohesive platoons. It is at the platoon level where esprit and morale develop, and the soldierization process takes place.[126]

Morale seems to be high in GIBT groups. In studies conducted by the ARI between 1993 and 1995, women in mixed-gender units reported higher morale. Male and female recruits have both said that they enjoy training together, which may make it easier to recruit people into the military. A 1997 study by the Rand Corporation showed that the majority of servicepeople in the study favored integrated basic training (75 percent of the women and 61 percent of the men). When the ARI studied people's attitudes regarding GIT, it found that females in mixed companies have higher levels of cohesion and teamwork. Companies made up of 75 percent males and 25 percent females seemed to produce the best mix.[127] Lieutenant Colonel Bob Frusha said, "I think the whole group is more cohesive when it is gender-integrated. If the males are in one company and they see the females in another company, they tend to think the grass is greener on the other side of the hill. Now that they are integrated, they've found that it is not."[128]

Captain James F. Amerault commanded a mixed-gender ship with 350 women on board. In 1993, he told Congress, "[I] never thought our readiness was found wanting because of the presence of women in the crew. I was never disappointed in the crew's performance, nor was there ever a time I thought the ship would have been better off with an all-male crew."[129]

Separating men and women is not an effective way to address problems that involve sexual misconduct.

Opponents of GIBT suggest that men and women should be separated for training and in certain other areas of the military to reduce problems that relate to sexual misconduct, including harassment. This is not only ineffective but tends to punish women for the inappropriate behavior of others, including men who engage in harassment.

Proper training led by well-qualified people who use effective techniques is a better and more long-term solution for such problems. From the top down, the military must avoid stereotyping, isolating, or devaluing women (who remain a minority in most military settings). Said Navy Rear Admiral Marsha Evans,

> The root of discriminatory behaviors, including sexual harassment, is an undervaluing of the contributions that women are making. They're not seen as full team players. You don't harass a full-fledged member of the team. There's a direct relationship between respect and acceptance and those behaviors.[130]

Firm rules and discipline are needed. Military rules concerning sexual behavior are far stricter than those in civilian life because of the need for discipline, trust, and teamwork among people who will serve together in vital missions. All of the service branches have instituted courses to educate personnel about harassment. In the wake of publicized incidents of harassment, they have also examined the subculture in the military, which traditionally included "macho" images of hard-drinking, woman-chasing servicemen.

Progress has been made as the military clarifies and enforces rules and provides education, sensitivity training, and mental health services. At the Army's Fort Wood, new trainees receive materials that explain in detail what kinds of behaviors are considered acceptable. Trainees of the opposite gender are not permitted to date, meet privately, exchange personal notes, or engage in any kind of sexual or intimate physical activities, including hugging. Women have repeatedly said that leadership is critical in fighting sexual misconduct and maintaining high morale. National Guard Sergeant Sharon Stallworth said, "It starts with the command. He sets the tone."[131] The commander of her unit, which experienced few sexual harassment problems, was Captain Torrey Hubred. Hubred said that he expected personnel to follow "three golden rules": "The first is to treat others the way you would be treated. The second is to make decisions you wouldn't be ashamed to see in the headlines tomorrow. And the third is ask, 'Would you do this if someone you love is watching?'"[132]

Observers say that, as base training continues, the genders become more accustomed to each other. When author Helen Rogan watched mixed-gender groups train at Fort McClellan, she noticed romantic activity and a degree of "sexual electricity" early in the training period but said that these elements later diminished. Rogan wrote, "They were behaving more and more like a team that happened to be made up of individual men and women, not opposing, polarized groups."[133]

Summary

Today's military relies on volunteers, and women will continue to play key roles in most, if not all, areas of the service branches. Since the 1970s, the trend is clearly toward more inclusion and integration, not less. Gender integration is a reality in education and training programs, as well as nearly every type of unit.

It seems unlikely that the Army, Navy, and Air Force will return to separate-gender training programs. Nonetheless, many Americans still bitterly oppose GIBT and want Congress and the Pentagon to discontinue it. Some even argue that gender-integrated training downgrades the preparation of combat troops, but this is fallacious because only men can enlist in the combat arms. These men complete both Basic and Advanced Individual Training in all-male units. No women take part in this process.

Opposition to gender-integrated training and service reflects arbitrary and conservative attitudes, along with resistance to change. Opponents ignore, or do not comprehend, the capabilities of women or the nature of today's gender-integrated military. With deep-rooted opinions on each side, this debate goes on.

Current Policies Regarding Motherhood Threaten National Security and American Society

O n March 23, 2003, during the war in Iraq, 30-year-old Shoshana Johnson, the single mother of a 2-year-old, was part of a U.S. Army maintenance unit that was ambushed and then captured after it made a wrong turn in the city of Nasiriyah. Johnson had originally signed on as an Army cook but now she was a prisoner of war (POW) with serious gunshot wounds in both legs. After U.S. troops freed her and six fellow soldiers on April 2, Johnson faced a long period of physical recovery and painful memories of captivity.

This situation is the predictable result of changes in military policies that affect mothers and families. As of 2006, mothers of young children could be deployed to war zones, where they might be captured or killed. In families in which both husband and wife are in the military, it is possible that both will be deployed at the same time.

Before 1975, women could not serve in the military at all if they had children. They were permitted to marry but were discharged if they became mothers through birth, adoption, or marriage. Executive Order 10240, signed by President Harry S. Truman in 1951, stated that the armed services must discharge women who had children under age 18 or who were stepmothers of children who lived in the household for more than 30 days per year. Pregnant women were required to leave the service. Some women who married divorced or widowed men with children could apply for waivers, but they were expected to prove that they could handle their dual responsibilities.

These policies recognized that women fulfill vital roles in raising their children and that military readiness is impaired if large numbers of servicemembers are nondeployable because of pregnancy or parenting duties. At that time, women with young children also found it impractical to remain in the military because there were no child-care facilities or other special benefits to assist mothers. Salaries were low, so paying for child care was not feasible. Also, historically, military personnel have been expected to aspire to standards of behavior that go beyond the standards in civilian life. Many Americans believe that taking no moral stand regarding the circumstances of pregnancy lowers those standards.

As people sought to change the restrictions regarding pregnancy and motherhood, both women and men pointed out

Executive Order 10240

Executive Order 10240 stated that "a woman who is pregnant or a mother should not be a member of the armed forces" and must instead "devote herself to the responsibilities she has assumed, remaining with her husband and child as a family unit."

potential problems. In 1977, Colonel Mary Halloren, who had served as staff director of the WAC in the European theater during World War II, said, "I feel very strongly that the military has got to be a ready and mobile force, and I can't see that it's a ready force with women who are pregnant or have small children."[134] Nonetheless, family policies changed dramatically after 1970 as the feminist movement gathered steam and new civil rights laws were passed.

By the time the Persian Gulf War began in 1990, thousands of mothers were in the active forces and reserves. The public became more aware of these women as the media showed them leaving for the Gulf. Soon the war was nicknamed the "Mommy War," even though more servicemen than servicewomen had children at that time. Critics called and wrote to the Pentagon to protest mothers' deployment. In some cases, both parents were serving in the Gulf, which meant that their children could be orphaned. Polls showed that most Americans thought that women with young children should not be sent to a war zone.

By the end of 1991, Congress had considered several bills that would bring home single parents or at least one member of a two-parent home in which both had been sent to the Gulf. After the war, President George H. W. Bush appointed a commission to study issues related to deployment of parents, especially mothers, to war zones. The commission recommended that the military not deploy single parents with preschool-age children to armed conflicts and that only one parent in a two-parent military family be deployed to a war zone.

The mid 1990s brought increasing acceptance of mothers in the service and major accommodations for pregnancy. As of 1995, the Navy permitted women to serve through the twentieth week of pregnancy, until deployment, if they were located within six hours of a medical facility. Pregnancy was to be regarded as a natural and "normal" event in the Navy, Army, and Air Force.

Liberal policies toward pregnancy disrupt military operations.

Before 1975, laws prevented pregnant women from remaining in the service. These laws were made, in part, to protect the health of women and their babies. They were also intended to keep pregnant women from being in positions in which they could not perform their jobs. Within two decades, these regulations and policies moved to the opposite extreme. This trend was apparent during the 1980s, when Navy personnel included twice as many single parents as were present in the civilian population. These people also tended to be married at a younger age. In 1992, 12.5 of the women on active duty were single parents.[135]

New policies of the Clinton era offered servicemembers numerous benefits in terms of housing, education, and health care. Free prenatal care and pediatric care, allowances for housing and dependents, subsidized child care, and career-training opportunities have drawn a disproportionate number of single mothers into the service. The number of single mothers in the military (34 percent of all military women) is more than twice as high as in the general population (12.7 percent), leading some critics to say that the military is running a giant day-care center. According to Elaine Donnelly, family-friendly policies "have created a perverse incentive for irresponsible behavior and single

THE LETTER OF THE LAW

Pregnancy Discrimination Act of 1978

This act amended Title VII of the Civil Rights Act of 1964, adding pregnancy to the list of ways in which people might face discrimination on the basis of gender. It bans discrimination against women because of pregnancy, childbirth, or related medical conditions.

parenthood, especially in the enlisted ranks. Instead of supporting stable families, such policies worsen non-deployability and readiness problems."[136]

As of 1995, military personnel cannot make pregnancy an issue or hinder a woman's career in any way on account of pregnancy. Servicewomen cannot be ordered to have pregnancy tests before they are deployed to a war zone. As a result, situations arise in which women must be evacuated from warships or battle zones, and some even give birth in these places. In 2003, a female Marine onboard a warship gave birth to a 7-pound infant while the ship was deployed near Kuwait. The 33-year-old Marine, a staff sergeant attached to a ground unit, claimed that she had not been aware that she was pregnant. The mother and baby were then evacuated to the United States. As Elaine Donnelly said, "This baby was born safely, despite obvious hazards, but childbirth aboard warships is not an acceptable situation."[137] Like others, Donnelly points out that pregnancy may be natural and normal, but that does not make it "normal" in war zones or on battleships. The Marine Corps attempts to

FROM THE BENCH

Frontiero v. Richardson (411 U.S. 677 1973)

Air Force Lieutenant Sharron Frontiero challenged a statute that said that wives of servicemen were automatically dependents but that servicewomen's husbands did not qualify for benefits unless they were dependent on their wives for more than half of their support.

The Court declared that this policy violated the due process clause of the Fifth Amendment because it treated women and men differently even though they were "similarly situated." In its decision, the Court said that this sex-based classification system involved "the very kind of arbitrary legislative choice forbidden by the Constitution."

prevent this situation by not permitting pregnant women to be deployed on ships at all.

The loss of personnel can seriously hinder military operations and waste resources. In numerous instances, pregnant women have been evacuated from naval vessels, beginning with the very first mixed-gender crew on the carrier USS *Dwight D. Eisenhower*, which left port in October 2004. Beforehand, 24 of the women who were originally assigned to the ship could not deploy because of pregnancy. During the month of January 2005, 5 women were evacuated because of pregnancy. Within a year, 39 women had been evacuated for that reason. On the USS *Cape Cod*, 200 of the 1,500 crew members were not deployed for medical reasons; 25 were pregnant. During the mid-1990s the Navy experienced a 10 percent pregnancy rate for women on six-month sea tours.

Clearly, when jobs are left vacant, a ship cannot function properly, especially a smaller vessel with fewer crew members available to rotate jobs. There is no guarantee that evacuated personnel can be replaced at all, let alone quickly. Morale declines and resentment increases when crew members must work extra hours because women were evacuated or relieved of duty because of pregnancy. Once pregnant women are removed from ships, their berths must be filled by other women because they are located in sections allocated for women.

Pregnant women require other accommodations. The service branches must be alert to jobs, materials, or settings that pose extra hazards for pregnant women and their unborn children. In 1997, the designers of a new amphibious assault ship called the LPD-17 were examining what they called appropriate "health criteria for pregnant sailors and Marines . . . for shipboard spaces."[138]

As a pregnancy continues, a woman servicemember may need to do increasingly lighter tasks or be reassigned. Pregnant women are exempted from normal routines, such as marching and field training. When they belong to a unit, restrictions on their activities and their absence for maternity leave causes adjustments and inconvenience for their units. Young single mothers also have higher rates of reporting late to work than other soldiers do. Dealing with these personnel problems distracts commanders and other personnel from the primary focus of the military.

Research shows that a significant number of women return to their military jobs with inadequate fitness levels after giving birth. In one study, Army women still had not returned to their prepregnancy fitness levels six to nine months after their babies were born. Women in this group were four times more likely to fail the Army Physical Fitness Test than other women soldiers. More than 33 percent were overweight according to military standards. The Army developed a special and compulsory physical training program just for postpartum women.

Policies toward pregnancy should be reevaluated, and some should be changed. The first step is to gather accurate and complete information about the impact of the social policies that were introduced during the 1990s. The Center for Military Readiness has asked Pentagon leaders to collect detailed statistics to show how many women have been unable to deploy or were evacuated from their units because of pregnancy. They have also suggested that the Department of Defense look at the data on all nondeployments and evacuations that occurred because of other medical problems and family or child care complications among dual-service couples and single parents with custody of their children.[139]

Policies must be revised so that they do not override military readiness and other important considerations. Phyllis Schlafly, an author and activist who opposes sending mothers to war, has said, "Pregnancy and motherhood are simply not compatible with military service. It is wrong to pretend that a woman who is pregnant or has a baby is ready to ship out to fight a war. She is not ready." Such policies, said Schlafly, go against "combat readiness, common sense and respect for family integrity."[140]

Sending mothers to war harms families and communities.

Americans recognize the vital roles that mothers play in family life. In poll after poll, the majority of Americans have said that they oppose the idea of mothers leaving babies and young children to go to war. A 1991 poll by the Associated Press found that 64 percent of Americans found it "unacceptable" to send women with young children into war zones.[141] When asked the same question about men, 28 percent said that was unacceptable.[142] In a 1992 Roper poll, 93 percent of Americans said that pregnant women should not serve in direct combat roles, and 69 percent said that single mothers should not do so.[143]

The wars in Afghanistan and Iraq marked the first time that a significant number of mothers had been deployed far from home for a long period of time. By July 2006, tens of thousands of American children had seen their mothers go to war. DoD statistics showed that 42.5 percent of all U.S. military personnel, including those in the National Guard and Reserves, had children, and about 33 percent of those children were under age five. Women in the military now are twice as likely as men to be single parents—about 24,000 of the approximately 213,059 women on active duty—so many of the women in war zones are their child's sole custodial parent. Married female soldiers are more likely than men to have children, and 29,000 married women on active duty have children.[144]

Forcing women to go to war, where they might be injured, tortured, raped, or killed seems especially horrific when they are mothers. For generations, societies have worked to elevate the role of mother and support the activities of bearing and raising children. Civilizations have made sacrifices on behalf of women and children. People who cherish the role of mother contend that it rips at the fabric of society to expose mothers, and therefore children, to mortal harm.

Children suffer when mothers are deployed to war, especially during the infancy and toddler stage, when they are most dependent on their mothers. In addition to missing their parent as they would with any absence, they may experience severe anxiety, fear, and depression. Researchers have identified a condition that they call "pediatric postwar syndrome," which involves various emotional and behavioral disorders, including sleep problems, discipline problems, and weaker attachments to their parents. As these children grow up, they may remain troubled in ways that cause problems for their communities.

Despite feminist claims, mothers and fathers are not interchangeable. Advocates of complete equality in the workplace contend that mothers are no more indispensable to their children than fathers or various caregivers. Other caregivers can do a good job, but they are not the same.

Deploying mothers to war zones is impractical.

Deploying mothers to war causes many practical problems as they leave home. Military couples and single parents are required to file Family Care Plans (FCPs) for both short- and long-term deployments, and the Navy requires plans for children or dependent parents. This system does not always work. During the Persian Gulf War, as people were deployed on short notice, the services found that many plans were outdated and children had no place to go. Some servicemembers had no plan in place because they had not filed the necessary papers.

Research has shown that, when troops are worried about their families, they have higher casualty rates. To maintain higher morale and performance, the military has increased the staff at family centers and mobilized people to give support to troops stationed away from their families. It offers mental health counseling services for children and the parents who are left behind, along with other practical assistance.

During the Persian Gulf War, some predictable problems occurred. Some women had to leave their units to return home for family emergencies, as did some men. One woman discovered that her in-laws were trying to gain permanent legal custody of her children by claiming that she was an unfit mother for going to war. She had to see to her defense in the lawsuit, which she eventually won, and then make new child care provisions. These kinds of problems could be prevented if women with custodial care of young children remain in nondeployable positions until the children reach at least school age.

Some people state that mothers must be assigned to war zones because of shortages in military personnel. Efficient recruitment and planning can prevent this problem. Military officials must recruit and train enough men to staff land-combat brigades, including those that collocate with combat troops, and avoid gender-based recruiting quotas that can lead to shortages of male soldiers.

Summary

Civilized nations protect mothers and children, and the United States should do likewise. The protection of women and children is traditionally a primary reason that nations go to war, and men have taken pride in defending their country, partly because of its women and children. This ideal is so important that is has been embodied in the Universal Declaration of Human Rights as Article 25: "Motherhood and childhood are entitled to special care and assistance," adopted December 10, 1948, by the General Assembly of the United Nations. Former WAC General Elizabeth Hoisington put it this way: "When the day comes that our women and children do not come first, our country is down the drain."[145]

Without question, women play vital roles in today's military and mothers need not be banned from the service outright, as they were before the 1970s. Current policies have become too permissive, however, and are hampering military efficiency as well as putting mothers in mortal danger. These policies favor notions of equality and career opportunity over military readiness. Although they purport to help women, these policies actually harm them, as well as their families and the nation as a whole.

Current Policies Toward Motherhood Are Fair Minded and Pragmatic

In September 1970, Air Force Captain Tommie Sue Smith, an Air Force attorney stationed in Washington, D.C., challenged Executive Order 10240 in court. Smith, a divorced mother, had been told that she could not take her eight-year-old son along to her new assignment in the Philippines. Air Force rules said that she could either leave her child behind or resign her commission. Instead, Smith filed a lawsuit, claiming that her rights were being violated under the equal protection clause of the Fourteenth Amendment.

Around that same time, Major Lorraine R. Johnson, a member of the Army Nurse Corps since 1958, faced the prospect of involuntary discharge after giving birth to her son. A member of the Army Reserve, Johnson spent 2,000 hours each year training medical corpsmen in intensive care and was 8 years shy of the 20-year requirement for full retirement. She would also lose $16,000 in reserve pay annually if she had to resign her commission. Johnson said that she was "ready, willing, and able" to perform her duties and that involuntary discharge violated her civil rights.[146]

After Johnson filed her lawsuit in district court, the Army granted her a "waiver" so that she could remain in the service. It began to issue similar waivers to other women. In Smith's case, the day after she filed her suit, the Air Force announced that it had changed its policy. Smith's case never went to court.

Smith and Johnson were among the many servicewomen who opposed policies that banned mothers from the service, signed into law in 1951. To continue their careers, some military women had even placed their children in boarding schools or gave up legal custody while still living with their children. Women could not take children with them to new assignments, yet divorced or widowed fathers in the service could.

Anna Flores faced involuntary discharge in 1970 because of long-standing policies toward pregnant women. Flores was a 23-year-old enlisted sailor stationed in Florida and engaged to marry a Navy enlisted man. Before they were married, she suffered a miscarriage. The Navy told her that she would be discharged on the grounds that she had been pregnant outside marriage. Letting her remain in the service "would imply that unwed pregnancy is condoned and would eventually result in a dilution of the moral standards set for women in the Navy."[147] Flores decided to fight the discharge. The American Civil Liberties Union (ACLU) filed a class action suit on behalf of Flores

THE LETTER OF THE LAW

Fifth Amendment Due Process Clause

"No person shall be ... deprived of life, liberty, or property, without due process of law; nor shall private property be taken for public use, without just compensation."

and all military women, alleging that they were being denied due process and equal protection of the law and that this policy violated their right to privacy. Women were being singled out for discharge, but servicemen who were involved in an unwed pregnancy could remain in the armed forces. To avoid a court battle, the Navy did not discharge Flores. Faced with similar situations, other service branches also let women remain.

These cases marked the onset of major policy changes that enabled women to continue their military careers while also bearing and raising children. Now that women are such an integral part of the military, these policies are not only more fair but essential to the mission of the military.

Policies must treat both genders equitably.

Before the 1970s, military policies toward pregnancy and motherhood were often illogical and discriminatory. They were based on antiquated ideas about proper gender roles that said that women belonged in the home. Determined servicewomen and their advocates worked for changes. By 1975, the service branches had officially lifted their bans on pregnant women and mothers.

In changing its policies, the military admitted that husbands and fathers did not face the same restrictions as women. Women were also singled out for penalties that did not apply to men; for example, single women who became pregnant or were known to have had abortions were dishonorably discharged. There was no logic to rules that discharged a woman for becoming a stepmother while allowing men to remain in the military regardless of their parenting responsibilities. Some men had been single parents for many years or had full custody of their children as a result of divorce, adoption, or widowhood. To automatically discharge women was discriminatory and showed no regard for their personal wishes or roles in the service.

The military must accommodate the conditions of pregnancy and motherhood and recognize pregnancy as a temporary condition. Otherwise, women cannot hope to attain equal opportunities in their military careers. Previous policies were designed to accommodate men only. Integrating women successfully required adjustments and new policies that take pregnancy into account.

Equality and fairness also dictate that women and men make similar sacrifices, including leaving their families when they are called to serve abroad. It is unfair to expect all fathers to serve if all mothers are automatically exempt. This would put extra burdens on men and show favoritism toward women, even though both join the all-volunteer army by choice. Servicemembers who do not want to be deployed to a war zone can choose career fields in the military that prevent that from happening. Those who enter deployable jobs know that they must be ready to go when they are called. As adults, whether parents or not, they make their own choices and do not require protection from groups outside the military.

Accommodations for motherhood are necessary and help, rather than harm, families.

New policies recognize that pregnancy is a normal process, not an illness, and that it does not affect all women in the same ways or impose the same limits on every woman. Years ago, people who wanted to ban women from certain jobs or military careers used the possibility of pregnancy and motherhood as excuses to exclude them. For example, in banning women from flying combat aircraft, members of Congress and the military warned that, because training was so costly, it would be wasted when these trained women pilots left the service because of pregnancy and motherhood. They exaggerated the way in which pregnancy and menstruation affect women, as for example in 1942, when Army planners called it a "physiological handicap which renders her [women in general] abnormal, unstable, etc. at certain times."[148]

Pregnancy is a reality when women are part of the military. Current policies recognize that reality and allow women time for maternity leave, after which they are expected to fulfill their commitments. Officials have learned to manage the situation by planning ahead and obtaining enough personnel so that units function smoothly and enough people are available for deployment.

Military policies protect servicewomen and their children in several significant ways. Pregnant servicewomen may remain on duty unless they require medical leave or their jobs pose special hazards to pregnant women. They are entitled to four to six weeks of maternity leave with no loss of rank, of salary, or of chances for promotion. Women who are about to be deployed can apply for deferments or hardship deferments if they have just given birth or have no viable child care options.

Current policies reflect the practical needs of the all-volunteer military.

The transition to a military with more families rather than mostly single or childless members evolved along with the change to an all-volunteer force. In previous decades, people were drafted and often served just two years. Now, more personnel have been signing up for longer tours of duty. Longer tours also help people learn and perform the highly technical jobs of the modern forces. People who remain in the service over a period of years are more likely to marry and have children along the way.

The military also makes an investment in training women who became proficient in their military careers. It would be impractical to discharge them abruptly if they wish to continue their careers after becoming mothers. Women may have skills that are critically needed.

Although there are strong arguments against sending mothers to war zones, military officials must be able to deploy the people they need when they need them. During the Gulf War, for example, President Bush, Defense Secretary Dick Cheney, and Chief of Staff Colin Powell pointed out the drawbacks of being able to deploy only one member of a two-parent military family.

They told Congress that this policy would weaken America's combat capability by removing key personnel. Cheney further stated that the purpose of the Department of Defense was "to be prepared to fight and win wars." He added, "We're not a social welfare agency."[149]

Deployability during the Gulf War was high among parents, which shows that including parents in the service did not impair military readiness. Less than one-half of one percent of the 23,000 single parents and 5,700 service couples with children had to be deferred from deployment for family reasons.[150] Their deployment rates were higher than the rates for unmarried men with no children.[151] If the military is barred from deploying large numbers of women because of motherhood, troop numbers might sag to a level that would require a draft. With a draft in place, both mothers and fathers could be exempt from going to war, but nobody has suggested reinstating that system.

Supporters of the family-friendly policies that were implemented during the 1990s point out that this kind of military attracts married recruits, and statistics show that married people create more stability. They have lower rates of drug and alcohol abuse and disciplinary problems. More people also will choose to reenlist if they appreciate the quality of life in the military. In light of these factors, it makes sense to offer family housing, child care, family activities, and counseling services for families and married couples in the service.

Children need not suffer serious emotional harm when mothers are deployed.

No definitive research is available to prove adverse effects on children when the mother goes to war. Some studies done during World War II focused on absent fathers. Examples of specific children in distress have been described, but this does not prove that all or most children will suffer serious or long-term psychological damage. Conversely, research has shown that children can bond with other loving, caring adults. Parenting roles can be filled by family members or trusted friends until a parent returns.

Fathers are no more expendable than mothers, and traditional gender roles have changed so that some men now stay home with children while their wives pursue careers, or both parents work outside the home and share parenting and household duties. One husband and father cared for an 11-month-old child and another child while also running the home and working full-time after his wife left for the Gulf. Of the experience, he said, "I know single dads can do as good a job as single moms. I know they can because I am doing it."[152]

A Naval commander in the Gulf said that most of the Red Cross messages that his crew received during their first two weeks at sea came from spouses back home who could not cope with being alone rather than from children of mothers serving in the Gulf.[153] An Air Force study found that children in traditional families with two parents and only one in the military showed more adjustment problems and signs of distress after the war than children of single parents or dual-career military couples.[154]

Women have said that, although they miss their children and love them very much, they are fighting for their children's benefit and doing the job they were trained to do. Many women believe that they are setting a good example for their children by fulfilling their obligations and serving their country.

Summary

Opponents to women in the military have long brought up women's physical characteristics, including pregnancy, as a way to keep them out of many—or even all—military jobs. Some of these people are well-intentioned and motivated by sincere concern for women and their families. Perhaps they also long for earlier times when roles were more rigid and predictable.

Obviously, the old military policies were too general and did not look at women as individuals, only as a class of people—an approach that is illogical as well as illegal. Like men, women train to serve, and feel strong patriotism and a call to duty. They are likewise able to carry out their military jobs and still fulfill their duties as parents.

Continuing
Debates

O ld debates continue and new ones arise as women enter more military roles and people seeking total gender integration try to eliminate the final barriers. In the Iraq war, thousands of women may eventually face combat situations during street fighting, rioting, terrorist attacks, and other operations. As a result of some work—as helicopter pilots, chemical warfare specialists, engineers, intelligence officers, logistics specialists, military police, and signal officers—more women may die or become POWs. What impact will that have on the debate over women in combat or mothers' roles in the military? Such debates are bound to continue, along with those that make up the remainder of this chapter.

The Collocation Policy

Laws in effect since 1994 ban women from serving "where units and positions are doctrinally required to physically collocate and remain with direct ground combat units that are closed to women." This policy was meant to ease fears when the DoD dropped the Risk Rule in 1994. Direct ground combat (DGC) units were still all male as of 2006.

Opponents of women in combat say that the military was sidestepping these rules during the Iraq war and did not notify Congress, as required by law. The Army assigned female soldiers to forward support companies, which collocate with direct ground combat troops at the battalion level. This practice is unlawful, say critics, and it increases burdens and risks for land combat soldiers. It can also confuse and upset troops, who are then expected to adjust to this change in accepted procedures. Female troops who are assigned to these units may not be physically capable of performing single-man rescues, should that be necessary, and other issues may arise when women are deployed with men.

For its part, the military said that these women would not see combat, but that, if that were to happen, women would be evacuated. Opponents call this plan unfeasible. In order to evacuate the 24 women who are part of these units, the military would have to use 2 Black Hawk helicopters, 6 Huey helicopters, 1 Chinook helicopter, 2 five-ton (or LMTV) trucks, or 12 up-armored HMMWVs (staffed by three people) and 4 to 6 unarmored HMMWVs. Critics say that using these valuable resources for evacuation purposes is both wasteful and impractical. Commanders would also need to ascertain exactly when combat begins in a place where the battle zones keep changing.

The Center for Military Readiness said that the Army must not use "semantics and sophistry to place female soldiers in units required to be all male."[155] The Center asked the chairmen of the House and Senate Armed Forces Committees to address this matter and asked the DoD to respond to a list of related questions. Among other things, the Center wants the DoD to ensure that women are not used in these units unless there is a verifiable and critical shortage of male troops for these positions. The DoD also should prove military necessity, clarify the legal aspects of collocation policies, and inform women of how these policies are being applied, said the Center.

This debate will likely continue as opponents argue that collocation disregards good military strategy and can lead to more loss of life. To those who oppose women in combat, collocation wrongly obscures the lines between combat and non-combat positions. Those on the other side argue that women are already in combat and that the policies should reflect that reality.

Selective Service and the Draft
Although the nation has an all-volunteer military, men still register with the Selective Service when they turn 18, in case a national emergency requires a draft. Should women also register? This has been the subject of debates and lawsuits.

Since its inception in World War I, the U.S. military draft has applied only to men. Women were not even allowed to help run Selective Service offices because officials thought that they would be offended by the questions men had to answer. This was in keeping with traditional ideas about women's roles and sensibilities. Although men were subject to the draft, many were exempted from service for various reasons. Before World War II, married men with dependents (a wife, children, or both) were exempt because even wives with jobs were considered "dependent." After the United States entered World War II in December 1941, men who married soon thereafter had to prove that their marriages were not shams to avoid service. The sequence for drafting men was as follows: single men without dependents, single men in non–war-related jobs with dependents, single men in war-related jobs with dependents, married men in non–war-related jobs with wives only, married men with both wives and children and no war-related job, and married men with wives and children and war-related jobs. A Selective Service Board memo dated June 23, 1942, said, "The necessity for giving adequate consideration to the family unit where a child or children are involved cannot be over emphasized," yet 71 percent of Americans favored drafting men with dependents if it was necessary to win the war.[156]

As the need for soldiers grew in 1942, some fathers were drafted and boards drafted men starting at age 18, partly to avoid drafting so many fathers. The draft law was revised in 1948 to defer husbands without children and then revised again during the Korean War in 1951 to defer only those with children unless a man proved that leaving home would cause extreme hardship. Deferments were available to college students throughout the 1960s, and many avoided service in Vietnam in that way.

During the early 1970s, the debate over a male-only draft flared when Congress passed the Equal Rights Amendment (ERA). Yet, the following year, the House Judiciary Committee declared that passing the ERA did not require drafting both men and women. (The ERA was not added to the Constitution because it was not ratified by two-thirds of the states.) In 1981, the Senate Armed Services Committee explained why women would not be subject to any draft: It noted that women make important contributions to combat support units but said that an induction system "that provided half men and half women to the training commands in the event of mobilization would be administratively unworkable and militarily disastrous."[157]

In the case of *Rostker v. Goldberg*, men challenged the male-only draft in the U.S. Supreme Court. The Court deferred to Congress, which stated that the draft is related to combat and thus women were ineligible.[158] Congress reiterated this position in 2003, after Congressman Charles Rangel (D-NY) introduced legislation that would have required young women to register for the draft.

That same year, another legal challenge was considered when *Schwartz v. Rascon* was filed in U.S. District Court in the District of Massachusetts. The plaintiff, with support from the American Civil Liberties Union, challenged the males-only provision for

Selective Service registration. District Judge Edward F. Harrington upheld the right of Congress to exempt women from registering for the Selective Service.

Around the world, laws and policies differ. Some countries have drafted women during times of emergency—for example, the Soviets and British during World War II. China, Eritrea, Israel, Libya, Malaysia, North Korea, Peru, and Taiwan draft women into their armies. Norwegian officials have discussed making military service compulsory for women in order to improve physical fitness, encourage more women to pursue military careers, and promote gender equality. In 2002, Sweden also considered female conscription on the grounds that excluding them goes against the ideal of equality.

Polls conducted since the 1970s show that most Americans oppose women being subjected to the draft. People who oppose

FROM THE BENCH

Rostker v. Goldberg (453 U.S. 57 1981)

This case began in 1971, when Robert Goldberg and some other men challenged the constitutionality of the male-only draft, saying that it violated their right to equal protection guaranteed by the Fifth Amendment. When the draft was discontinued in 1972, the case became moot. It became relevant again in 1980, after the Soviet Union invaded Afghanistan. President Carter asked Congress for permission to revive Selective Service registration in case the nation had to go to war, and he requested funds to register both men and women. Congress approved registering only men, a process that began in July 1980. By then a class action suit, the case reached the Supreme Court in 1981. In the decision, Justice William Rehnquist noted the purpose of the registration—to draft people for combat—and stated that men and women were not similarly situated in regard to the draft because "women as a group, unlike men as a group, are not eligible for combat." Rehnquist reasoned that "the Constitution requires that Congress treat similarly situated persons similarly, not that it engage in gestures of superficial equality."

women serving in combat point out that, if that ban is lifted, women can expect to be required to register for a possible draft with men.

Women at Military Academies

Before 1976, women were denied entry to the nation's military academies, regardless of their qualifications, because of gender. Members of Congress who pushed for gender-integrated academies found support in various laws, including the Equal Pay Act of 1963, Title VII of the Civil Rights Act of 1964, the Equal Employment Opportunity Act, Title IX of the Educational Amendment, and the ERA. After Congress passed the ERA, it

THE LETTER OF THE LAW

Public Law 94-106

Public Law 94-106 signed in 1975, opened military academies to women beginning in 1976.

Section 803(a) of Public Law 94-106 states that:

Notwithstanding any other provision of law, in the administration of chapter 403 of title 10, United States Code (this chapter) (relating to the United States Military Academy), chapter 603 of such title (relating to the United States Naval Academy), and chapter 903 of such title (relating to the United States Air Force Academy), the Secretary of the military department concerned shall take such action as may be necessary and appropriate to insure that (1) female individuals shall be eligible for appointment and admission to the service academy concerned, beginning with appointments to such academy for the class beginning in calendar year 1976, and (2) the academic and other relevant standards required for appointment, admission, training, graduation, and commissioning of female individuals shall be the same as those required for male individuals, except for those minimum essential adjustments in such standards required because of physiological differences between male and female individuals.

was ratified in 33 states but was never made into law. Public Law 94-106, however, forced military academies to admit women. As of 1996, women have been admitted to and have graduated from the United States Military Academy (West Point); the U.S. Naval Academy; the Air Force Academy; and the Coast Guard Academy. During the 1990s, women filed lawsuits to gain admission to the Citadel and the Virginia Military Institute, both of which receive public as well as private funding. The Supreme Court upheld their right to attend the schools, and women have graduated from both institutions.

The first women at the academies faced a great deal of ridicule, anger, and rejection from male cadets, as well as families of male cadets, local communities, and alumni. Some people continue to say that women do not belong there. In her book *Ground Zero*, author Linda Francke discussed the "cultural hostility" toward women that can still be felt in aspects of academy life.[159] Opponents say that the presence of women has diluted the quality of physical training, ruined the rugged atmosphere, and shattered old traditions: Military academies dropped the practice of "peer ratings" because women's scores were far below men's, and cadets now wear running shoes instead of combat boots because women had more injuries while wearing boots. Certain exercises that require significant upper-body strength were eliminated, as was the "recondo" endurance week at West Point because women found it too strenuous to march long distances with a full backpack. Opponents also say that women take spots away from men who could be training for combat and combat leadership. Here again, the combat exclusion policy enters the discussion.

Supporters say that female candidates are at least as qualified as males. Between 1976 and 1992, a higher proportion of women who entered West Point were National Honor Society members in high school and had graduated first or second in their classes. More female than male cadets were selected as Rhodes and Marshall scholars.[160] In West Point's classes of 1990 and 1991, 68 and

64 percent of the women seniors made the dean's list, compared to 52 and 56 percent of the men.[161]

As for physical strength and endurance, not all military men are expected to meet the same standards, either. Opponents tend to focus on physical capabilities rather than looking at all of the qualifications that cadets bring to the table. The military needs people who can fill a multitude of roles, including many that rely more on cognitive skills than on physical ability.

Some people say that women have made the academies better by adding a new perspective. They have also helped officials become more aware of problems that arose from certain traditions, such as hazing by upperclassmen. Some of these traditions serve no useful purpose for women or for men, and do not promote a more effective military force.

Supporters of women at the academies believe that they can produce outstanding leaders without the male bonding rituals that were common before women were admitted. Both women and men can keep their gender identities as they complete their studies and training. Giving women a chance to compete for spots in the nation's academies and in other military positions shows a commitment toward equal opportunity. It creates a framework whereby women can receive officer training and compete more fairly for assignments and promotions.

Sexual Misconduct

During the mid-1990s, the military dealt with sexual misconduct scandals at two Army bases (Aberdeen and Fort Leonard Wood); at the Great Lakes Naval Training Station in Illinois; and at Lackland Air Force Base in Texas. A drill sergeant and a company commander were among those charged with rape at one Army base. Allegations of rape, harassment, and fraternization forced the armed services to take yet another look at the problem of sexual misconduct in the military. Sexual misconduct, including harassment, has been a recurring problem in every service branch and predates the integration of women into the armed

Marine Lance Corporal Megan L. Phuhl searches an Iraqi woman in Baghdad. In Iraq, if female civilians are to be searched, the search must be performed by a female soldier.

forces. In 1987, the Pentagon released a report that stated that sexual harassment, ranging from verbal abuse to molestation, was pervasive. When Senator Sam Nunn called for an investigation in

1990, he said that reports of misconduct in the Navy suggested that it arose from "institutional problems in the Navy and its treatment of women."[162]

In 1997, the Joint Task Force for Sexual Assault Prevention and Response offered recommendations, including clear definitions of sexual assault and harassment, more support for victims, and more training and education on the subject for all personnel. In 1988, Pentagon studies showed that 64 percent of all military women reported having been subjected to some kind of sexual harassment. That number went down slightly, to 55 percent, in the late 1990s.[163]

People agree that sexual misconduct is unacceptable but sometimes disagree about how to address it. Some people continue to recommend separating men and women into single-gender training programs. They believe that, as long as the military continues to integrate the sexes in every way, they will be forced to monitor and regulate sexual activities, which will drain time, energy, and monetary resources. They also worry about the impact that false allegations can have on people's careers. In response, other people note that the Marines have had higher rates of reported sexual harassment than other service branches even though they operate single-gender boot camps. Recently, more people have pointed out that the rules are already in place—but leaders need to make sure that they are enforced. Said former Assistant Secretary of the Navy Barbara Pope, "What's critical are the informal rules." Pope also has suggested that the military offer women practical and effective ways to stop harassment.[164]

Women continue to say that effective leadership is vital. According to Major Andrea Hollen, U.S. Army (Ret.), the first woman to graduate from West Point:

> The drill instructor is clearly in a position of authority, and there's absolutely no excuse for the behavior exhibited at Aberdeen. And I do believe very strongly that leadership can

make a difference. . . . The military is not some kind of out of control mob. And if soldiers feel that their leaders take a personal interest in them [and] if their leaders have the charisma to really align the unit around its mission and focus on readiness, it can make a tremendous difference.[165]

Women on Submarines?

As of 2006, women were still not eligible for submarine duty, although some people disagree with that policy. Through the years, women overcame enormous barriers to gain billets at sea. In doing so, they faced not only the usual arguments but also old prejudices and myths about women being "bad luck" on a ship. When the 1948 law to admit women into the services was being debated in Congress, Carl Vinson (D-GA) expressed the

"Women Don't Belong"

As recently as 1990, the Update Report on the Progress of Women in the Navy concluded that the Navy as an institution had the attitude that "women don't belong because they haven't the physical strength and stamina, the psyche, or the 'killer instinct' needed to fight the enemy" and "are perceived as distanced from the heart of the organization and its primary mission-achieving units." It went on to say:

This mentality often rejects women as "distractors" [sic] from the business at hand and as "time takers" who burden the system either with their aspirations for equality or their inability to handle their "personal problems" (e.g. pregnancy). "It would be a lot easier if women weren't here" is a favorite expression of the traditional image upholder, as is the alternative pronouncement that "Women are to be protected, not to sail in harm's way, and any woman who would want to do the latter is abnormal."

Source: *Update Report on the Progress of Women in the Navy.* Prepared by the 1990 Navy Women's Study Group. Washington, D.C., 1990.

feelings of many when he said, "Just fix it so they cannot go to sea at all."[166]

Women did finally go to sea in the 1970s. During the 1990s, they became eligible for duty on combat vessels, but submarines are still off limits. Periodically, the Navy has examined this possibility and called for reports that show how such a plan might be implemented. This happened in 2000, for example, and again in 2006, when Navy leaders said that they were giving the matter serious consideration. Pentagon rules require the Navy to notify Congress if it intends to assign female sailors to submarines. Congress can either approve or reject such a plan.

Opponents point out that life on a submarine is far more confined and difficult than life on a regular ship, as crews of 130 spend six months living in a space no larger than a medium-sized home. Facilities are tight, with one shower per 50 people and about 40 percent of the crew members sharing the same bunk by sleeping in shifts. The costs of building and maintaining separate berths and bathing facilities for men and women on these vessels would be high. Other concerns involve the poor air quality and toxic substances circulating in a closed vessel, because these would pose a threat to women of childbearing age who might be pregnant. Adults can handle the level of carbon monoxide in the submarine, but it could be hazardous for a fetus. If a pregnant woman had to be evacuated, a commander would face difficult choices because submarine missions are secret. An evacuation can also be dangerous because it requires a helicopter to lower a basket down to the sub, a difficult task in the best of circumstances.

DACOWITS and others who advocate opening submarine duty to women say that it is unfair to close this career path. They point out that some women are willing to live with the inconvenience and discomfort of submarine life and have the physical strength and skills for these jobs. Women have said that they would volunteer for submarine duty. One approach is to demand exactly that they meet the same requirements as men for submarine duty, with no exceptions. This would not alleviate the cost, however—an estimated $300,000 to provide facilities for each woman on a sub.

A third alternative has been suggested: submarines with all-female crews. Navy women themselves have said that few women have enough upper-body strength to perform all of the heavy labor on these vessels, however.

Summary

There are no easy answers to questions about women in the military—the arguments reflect deep-rooted beliefs and often become emotional. Both sides cite statistics, official reports, experts, firsthand observations, philosophical ideas, and anecdotal evidence to support their positions. Congress, members of the military, and the public are still seeking to find an optimal balance of military readiness, equal opportunity, and social values.

Introduction: Changing Roles for Women

1. Quoted in Linda Bird Francke, *Ground Zero: The Gender Wars in the Military.* New York: Simon & Schuster, 1997, p. 59.

2. Quoted in Abby Wettan Kleinbaum, *The War Against the Amazons.* New York: New Press/McGraw Hill, 1983, p. 131ff.

3. Quoted in Arlene Eisen Bergman, *Women of Viet Nam.* San Francisco: People's Press, 1975, p. 54.

4. Jean Markale, *Women of the Celts.* London: Gordon Cremnes, 1972, p. 38.

5. Seymour Reit, *Behind Enemy Lines: The Incredible Story of Emma Edmonds, Civil War Spy.* San Diego, Calif.: Harcourt, Brace, Jovanovich, 1988.

6. Katharine Jones, *Heroines of Dixie,* Westport, Conn.: Greenwood Press, 1955, p. xxxi.

7. Mattie E. Treadwell, *The Women s Army Corps.* Washington, D.C.: Government Printing Office, 1954, p. 4.

8. E.S. Hughes (Major, General Staff), approved by B. G. Campbell King (Assistant Chief of Staff), "Memorandum for the Assistant Chief of Staff, G-1. Subject: Participation of Women in War," September 21, 1928.

9. Major General Jeanne Holm, USAF (Ret.), *Women in the Military: An Unfinished Revolution.* Rev. ed. Novato, Calif.: Presidio Press, 1992, p. 20.

10. *U.S. Congress Congressional Record* 87 (May 28, 1941): p. 4693.

11. Quoted in John Costello, *Love Sex and War—Changing Values, 1939–1945.* London: Collins, Grafton Street, 1985, p. 64.

12. Doris Weatherford, *American Women and World War II.* New York: Facts On File, 1990, p. 30.

13. Judith Bellafaire, *The Women's Army Corps in World War II.* U.S. Center of Military History. Available online at http://www.army.mil/cmh-pg/brochures/wac/wac.htm. Also discussed in Leisa D. Meyer, "Creating a Women's Corps: Public Response to the WAAC/WAC and Questions of Citizenship," in Paula Nassen Poulos, ed., *A Women's War Too: Women in the Military in World War II.* Washington, D.C.: National Archives and Records Administration, 1996.

14. Quoted in Office of the Chief of Military History (OCMH), *Report of the General Board, U.S. Forces, European Theater. Study of the Women's Army Corps in the European Theater of Operations.* Vol. I, p. 11.

15. Quoted in Chuck Lawliss, *The Marine Book: A Portrait of America's Military Elite.* London: Thames & Hudson, 1988.

16. Quoted in R.P. Ward and C.J. Doherty, "History of the 2563d Army Air Forces Base unit, Avenger Field, Sweetwater, Texas, 1 November 1944 to 20 December 1944." pp. 94–95.

17. Holm, *Women in the Military,* p. 157.

18. House Armed Services Committee, *Report of the House Armed Services Committee on H. R. 5894* (1967), quoted in Holm, *Women in the Military,* p. 201.

Point: Restrictions Against Women in Combat Should Remain in Place

19. Women's Research & Education Institute-WREI, 1991:9; U.S. General Accounting Office/NSIAD, 99-7, October 1998.

20. See Nancy Loring Goldman, ed., *Female Soldiers: Combatants Or Noncombatants?* Westport, Conn.: Greenwood Press, 1982, p. 247.

21. Ibid.

22. Mackubin Thomas Owens, "GI Janes, By Stealth," *National Review,* December 27, 2004. Available online at http://www.nationalreview.com/owens/owens200412090818.asp.

23. *Presidential Commission on the Assignment of Women in the Armed Services Report to the President.* Washington, D.C.: U.S. Government Printing Office, 1993.

24. "Israeli Women Won't See Combat," WorldNetDaily, October 20, 2003. Available online at www.worldnetdaily.com/news/article.asp?ARTICLE_ID=35170.

25. Helen Rogan, *Mixed Company: Women in the Modern Army*. New York: G.P. Putnam's Sons, 1981, p. 65.

26. Lisa Zagaroli, "Leaders Are Focus of Reform Efforts," *Detroit News*, July 11, 2004. Available online at http://detnews.com/2004/project/0407/13/a01-208481.htm.

27. David Horowitz, "The Feminist Assault on the Military," *National Review*, October 2, 1992, p. 46.

28. Kirsten Scharnberg, "Stresses of Battle Hit Female GIs Hard: VA Study Hopes to Find Treatment for Disorder," *Chicago Tribune*, March 20, 2005.

29. Kate O'Beirne, *Women Who Make the World Worse and How Their Radical Feminist Assault Is Ruining Our Families, Military, Schools, and Sports*. New York: Penguin, 2006, p. 125.

30. The Council on Biblical Manhood and Womanhood, "Women in Combat: A Resolution," 2005. Available online at www.cbmw.org/resources/articles/combat.php.

31. Quoted in E.A. Blacksmith, ed., *Women in the Military*. New York: H. W. Wilson, 1992, p. 26.

32. Quoted in Francke, *Ground Zero*, p. 253.

33. Quoted in "Women's Combat Role on Front Burner," *The Atlanta Journal-Constitution*, June 27, 2005. Available online at http://www.military.com/NewsContent/0,13319,FL_women_062705,00.html.

34. John Hillen, "The Real Heroes Aren't on TV," *The Wall Street Journal*, December 20, 2001.

35. Quoted in Dr. Gerald L. Atkinson, CDR USN (Ret.), "War as Entertainment: War as Radical Feminist Propaganda," March 4, 2002. Available online at http://www.newtotalitarians.com/WarAsEntertainment.html.

36. Andrea Stone, "They're 'Not An Experiment Anymore' " *USA Today*, January 11, 2002.

37. Atkinson, "War as Entertainment," http://www.newtotalitarians.com/WarAsEntertainment.html.

38. Ibid.

39. O'Beirne, *Women Who Make the World Worse*, p. 123.

40. *Presidential Commission on the Assignment of Women in the Armed Services Report to the President*. Washington, D.C.: U.S. Government Printing Office, 1993, p. C-80. Also discussed in Richard A. Gabriel and Paul L. Savage, *Crisis in Command: Mismanagement in the Army*. New York: Hill & Wang, 1979.

41. Philip Carter, "War Dames," *Washington Monthly*, December 2002. Available online at http://www.washingtonmonthly.com/features/2001/0212.carter.html.

42. O'Beirne, *Women Who Make the World Worse*, p. 122.

43. Quoted in Cynthia Enloe, *Does Khaki Become You? The Militarisation of Women's Lives*. London: Pandora Press, 1988, pp. 153–154.

44. Lee Bockhorn, "Women at Arms," Policy *Review*, August 2000. Available online at http://www.policyreview.org/aug00/Bockhorn.html.

45. Owens, "GI Janes," http://www.nationalreview.com/owens/owens200412090818.asp.

46. O'Beirne, *Women Who Make the World Worse*, p. 122.

47. Rowan Scarborough, "Pregnant Troops Leave the War; Central Command Not Counting," *Washington Times*, June 15, 2004. Available online at http://washingtontimes.com/national/20040615-115647-8125r.htm.

48. Ibid.

49. Quoted in Mackubin T. Owens, "Mothers in Combat Boots," *The Human Life Review* (Spring 1997): pp. 35–45.

50. Quoted in Rowan Scarborough, "Report Leans Toward Women in Combat," *The Washington Times*, December 13, 2004.

51. O'Beirne, *Women Who Make the World Worse*, p. 117; discussed in U.S. Military Image Study, August 4, 2004.

52. "Women in Combat. Report to the President," in *Presidential Commission on the Assignment of Women in the Armed Services Report to the President*. Washington,

D.C.: U.S. Government Printing Office, 1993.

53. Quoted in George Neumayr, "Collocating Coffins," *American Spectator*, March 18, 2005. Available online at http://www.spectator.org/dsp_article.asp?art_id=7911.

54. Stephanie Gutmann, *The Kinder, Gentler Military: Can America's Gender-Neutral Fighting Force Still Win Wars?* New York: Scribner, 2000.

55. Brian Mitchell, *Women in the Military: Flirting With Disaster*. Washington, D.C.: Regnery, 1998.

56. Stephanie Gutmann, *The Kinder, Gentler Military*.

Counterpoint: Women Should Be Eligible to Serve in Ground Combat

57. Quoted in Sergeant Sara Wood, U.S. Army Press Service, "Military Woman Receives Silver Star." Available online at http://userpages.aug.com/captbarb/silverstar.html.

58. Quoted in Francke, *Ground Zero*, p. 71.

59. Molly M. Ginty, "Record Number of Female Soldiers Fall," *Women's Enews*, March 20, 2005. Available online at http://www.womensenews.org/article.cfm/dyn/aid/2226/context/cover/.

60. David E. Jones, *Women Warriors*, p. 249.

61. Ibid., p. 93.

62. Quoted in Francke, *Ground Zero*, p. 247.

63. Quoted in Elizabeth Stone, *Women of the Cuban Revolution*. New York: Pathfinder Press, 1981, p. 7.

64. Quoted in Eva Isaksson, ed., *Women and the Military System*. New York: St. Martin's Press, 1988, p. 190.

65. Quoted in Sally Hayton-Keeva, *Valiant Women*. San Francisco: City Lights Book, 1987, p. 1.

66. Quoted in Francke, *Ground Zero*, p. 71.

67. Quoted in Amy Nathan, *Count On Us: American Women in the Military*. Washington, D.C.: National Geographic, 2004, p. 73.

68. Carter, "War Dames," Available online at http://www.washingtonmonthly.com/features/2001/0212.carter.html.

69. Quoted in Susan Dominus, "The Deadliest Day for Women," *Glamour*, June 2006.

70. Francke, *Ground Zero*, p. 248.

71. See Betsy Pisik, "Military Women Exercise Power Potential," *Working Woman*, July–August 1996, p. 20.

72. Discussed in Pisik, "Military Women," p. 20; Soraya Nelson, "Training Program Toughens Women to Handle Army's Men-Only Jobs," *Army Times*, February 12, 1996, p. 3.

73. Rogan, *Mixed Company*, p. 69.

74. Jones, *Women Warriors*, p. 250.

75. Quoted in Jean Zimmerman, *Tailspin: Women at War in the Wake of Tailhook*. New York: Doubleday, 1995, p. 217.

76. Freda Adler, *Sisters in Crime: The Rise of the Female Criminal*. Waveland Press, 1975.

77. Robert Briffault, *The Mothers*, 1927.

78. Rogan, *Mixed Company*, p. 90.

79. Quoted in Rogan, *Mixed Company*, p. 91.

80. Ibid.

81. Quoted in Holm, *Women in the Military*, p. 237.

82. Donna St. George, "Female Veterans Battle With Stress Syndrome: Doctors Studying Effects on Women," *Washington Post*, August 21, 2006.

83. Elizabeth Vaughan, "Community Under Stress," cited in *Presidential Commission on the Assignment of Women in the Armed Forces*. Issued November 1992, p. 233.

84. Quoted in "A Woman's Burden," *Time*, March 28, 2003 (from interview with Cathy Booth Thomas, 1992, http://www.time.com/time/nation/article/0,8599,438760,00.html).

85. Quoted in Francke, *Ground Zero*, p. 78.

86. Quoted in Zimmerman, *Tailspin* p. 280.

87. *United States v. Virginia* 518 US 515 (1996).

88. Quoted in Zimmerman, *Tailspin*, pp. 280–281.

89. Jones, *Women Warriors*, pp. xi, xii.

90. Holm, *Women and the Military*, p. 257.

91. Jake Willens, "Women in the Military: Combat Roles Considered." Center for Defense Information (CDI), August 7, 1996, *Minerva* Spring 1994. Available online at http://www.cdi.org/issues/women/combat.html.

92. "Dissent from the Recommendation on the Exclusion of Women from Combat Aircraft," in *Presidential Commission on the Assignment of Women in the Armed Services Report to the President*. Washington, D.C.: U.S. Government Printing Office, 1993, p. 85.

93. America's Defense Monitor (Hosted by Admiral Gene LaRocque), "Women Warriors," February 28, 1993. Transcript available online at http://www.cdi.org/adm/Transcripts/624/.

94. Quoted in Holm, *Women in the Military*, p. 463.

95. Vicki Nielsen, "Women in Uniform." *NATO Review* 49 (Summer 2001). Available online at www.nato.int/docu/review/2001/0102-09.htm.

96. Zimmerman, *Tailspin*, pp. 140–141. *Presidential Commission on the Assignment of Women in the Armed Forces, Excerpts From the Hearings*. Prepared by R. Cort Kirkwood, Media Liaison, Department of Communications and Congressional Affairs. 1992.

97. Interviewed in Broadcast: America's Defense Monitor (Hosted by Admiral Gene LaRocque), "Women Warriors," February 28, 1993. Transcript available online at http://www.cdi.org/adm/Transcripts/624/.

Point: Gender-integrated Training and Units Offer No Benefits and Impair Military Readiness

98. Stephanie Gutmann, *The Kinder, Gentler Military*.

99. R.D. Gersh, "Army to Return to Single-Sex Companies in Boot Camps," May 4, 1982.

100. *Presidential Commission on the Assignment of Women in the Armed Services Report to the President*. Washington, D.C.: U.S. Government Printing Office, 1993.

101. Report of the Federal Advisory Committee on Gender Integrated Training and Related Issues to the Secretary of Defense (Kassebaum-Baker Report). p. 15. December 16, 1997.

102. Rowan Scarborough, "Pentagon Pressed to Separate Sexes in Basic Training," *Washington Times*, August 7, 2001, p. A-1.

103. *Final Report of the Congressional Commission on Military Training and Gender-Related Issues*. 1(July 1999): p. 124.

104. *Report of the Presidential Commission on the Assignment of Women in the Armed Forces*. Issued in November 1992.

105. David Horowitz, *The Feminist Assault on the Military*. Studio City, Calif.: Center for the Study of Popular Culture, 1992, p. 16.

106. Stephanie Gutmann, "The Great Umbrella Debate," *The New York Times*, October 9, 1997, p. A39.

107. See Ian M.M. Gemmell, "Injuries Among Female Army Recruits." *Journal of the Royal Society of Medicine* (2002): pp. 23–27. Available online at http://www.jrsm.org/cgi/content/abstract/95/1/23; and Nigel Hawkes, "Equal Opportunity Damages Health of Women Soldiers," *London Times*, January 3, 2002.

108. Quoted in "For Marines, Separate Training Is What Works," *USA Today*, September 15, 1997, p. A18.

109. Horowitz, *Feminist Assault*, p. 16.

110. Larry Lane (SFC), "Getting the Right Mix," *Soldiers* 50 (March 1995). Available online at http://www.army.mil/soldiers/march95/p13.htm.

111. Senior Review Panel, *Report on Sexual Harassment*, Vols. I and II. Released September 11, 1997, pp. A-19, A-29.

112. Quoted in Roscoe Bartlett, "Single-Sex Training Is Best for Men and Women," *Air Force Times*, June 9, 1997, p. 28.

113. USA Operational Medical Research Program, "Bone Health and Military Medical Readiness." Military Operational Medicine Research Program (MOMRP). Available online at http://www.momrp.org/70.htm.

114. "1999 Military Operational Medicine Research Program," MOMRP, USARMRC, and "Summary Report: Workshop Research on Physical Fitness Standards and Measurements Within the Military Services (1999)."

115. Stephanie Gutmann, "Sex and the Soldier," *The New Republic,* February 24, 1997, p. 19.

116. Stephanie Gutmann, *The Kinder, Gentler Military.*

Counterpoint: Training and Service Should Be Gender Integrated

117. Quoted in "Radcliffe Indeed—Girl Aims to Enter Annapolis," *New York Times,* October 24, 1956, p. 37.

118. Quoted in "Statement of Nancy Duff Campbell, Co-President National Women's Law Center, Before the Subcommittee on Personnel, Committee on Armed Services U.S. Senate on Gender-Integrated Training," June 5, 1997.

119. Statement of Brigadier General Evelyn "Pat" Foote, US Army (Ret.), Before the House National Security Military Personnel Subcommittee Concerning the Report of the Federal Advisory Committee on Gender Integrated Training and Related Issues (Kassebaum-Baker Report), p. 99.

120. U.S. Army Research Institute. GAO/T-NSIAD-97-174 and GAO/Larry Lane, "Basic Training—Together," *Soldiers,* March 1995, Vol. 50, No. 3 http://www.army.mil/soldiers/march95/p13.htm.

121. *Basic Training: Services Are Using a Variety of Approaches to Gender Integration,* U.S. General Accounting Office (GAO), Report to the Chairman, Subcommittee on Military Personnel, Committee on National Security, House of Representatives. Issued in June 1996.

122. Lane, "Basic Training," http://www.army.mil/soldiers/march95/p13.htm.

123. *Basic Training: Services Are Using a Variety of Approaches to Gender Integration.* U.S. GAO, "Gender Issues: Improved Guidance and Oversight Are Needed to Ensure Validity and Equity of Fitness Standards." *Report to the Ranking Minority Member, Subcommittee on Readiness, Committee on Armed Services, U.S. Senate,* November 1998.

124. Lane, "Basic Training," http://www.army.mil/soldiers/march95/p13.htm.

125. Rogan, *Mixed Company,* p. 91.

126. Statement of Brigadier General Foote, (Kassebaum-Baker Report), March 17, 1998.

127. Lane, "Basic Training," http://www.army.mil/soldiers/march95/p13.htm.

128. Quoted in Lane, "Basic Training," http://www.army.mil/soldiers/march95/p13.htm.

129. Quoted in Laurie Weinstein and Christie White, *Wives and Warriors: Women and the Military in the United States and Canada.* Bergin & Garvey, 1997, p. 87.

130. Quoted in Zimmerman, *Tailspin,* p. 180.

131. Quoted in Pamela Martineau and Steve Wiegand, "Sexual Combat," *Sacramento Bee,* March 7, 2005. Available online at http://dwb.sacbee.com/content/news/projects/women_at_war/story/12523663p-13379149c.html.

132. Ibid.

133. Rogan, *Mixed Company,* p. 101.

Point: Current Policies Regarding Motherhood Threaten National Security and American Society

134. Quoted in Francke, *Ground Zero,* p. 105.

135. *Panel Three Report to the U.S. Presidential Commission on the Assignment of Women to the Armed Forces.* Issued November 15, 1992, p. 46.

136. Quoted in Center for Military Readiness (CMR), "Baby Born on Warship." June 12, 2003. Available online at http://www.cmrlink.org/social.asp?docID=191.

137. Ibid.

138. Owens, "Mothers in Combat Boots," pp. 35–45.

139. CMR, "Baby Born on Warship," http://www.cmrlink.org/social.asp?docID=191.

140. Quoted in Carol Wekesser and Matthew Polesetsky, eds., *Women in the Military* San Diego, Calif.: Greenhaven Press, 1991.

141. O'Beirne, *Women Who Make the World Worse,* p. 124.

142. Associated Press Poll, February 20, 1991, cited in Martineau and Wiegand, "Fractured Families," *Sacramento Bee*, March 9, 2005.

143. Roper Organization, Inc. "Attitudes Regarding the Assignment of Women in the Armed Forces: The Military Perspective," September 1992.

144. Kate O'Beirne, *Women Who Make the World Worse.*

145. Rogan, *Mixed Company*, p. 24.

Counterpoint: Current Policies Toward Motherhood Are Fair Minded and Pragmatic

146. Holm, *Women and the Military*, p. 297.

147. Quoted in "A Double Standard in the Navy," *Washington Post*, August 25, 1970.

148. Quoted in Treadwell, *The Women's Army Corps*, p. 4.

149. Quoted in Martineau and Wiegand, "Fractured Families," Sacramento Bee, March 9, 2005.

150. Shirley Sagawa and Nancy Duff Campbell, *Recommendations to the Presidential Commission on the Assignment of Women in the Armed Forces Regarding Parents in Military Service.* Washington D.C.: National Women's Law Center, November 14, 1992.

151. U.S. General Accounting Office, *Women in the Military—Deployment in the Persian Gulf War.* GAO/NSIAD-92-93, July 1993, p. 52.

152. Quoted in James Thornton, "When Minnesota Moms Go to War," *Minnesota Monthly*, March 1991, p. 66.

153. Francke, *Ground Zero*, p. 147.

154. "A Study of the Effectiveness of Family Assistance Programs in the Air Force During Operations Desert Shield/ Storm." Executive Summary, Contract Number F49642-88-D0003.

Conclusion: Continuing Debates

155. Center for Military Readiness (CMR), "Questions About Pentagon Violations of Policy and Law," March 1, 2006. Available online at http://cmrlink.org/WomenInCombat.asp?docID=262.

156. George Q. Flynn, *The Draft, 1940–1973.* Kansas City: University Press of Kansas, 1993, pp. 69–70.

157. Ibid.

158. *Rostker v. Goldberg* 453 U.S. 57 (1981).

159. See Francke, *Ground Zero*, Chapter 7: The Underground World at the Academies.

160. Francke, *Ground Zero*, p. 198.

161. *Report on the Integration and Performance of Women at West Point for the Defense Advisory Committee on Women in the Services [DACOWITS].* February 1992, p. 23.

162. Timothy Noah, Richard J. Newman, Bruce B. Auster, Katia Hetter, and David Fischer, "Dishonoring the U.S. Uniform/Why the Army takes misconduct very seriously," *U.S. News & World Report*, November 25, 1996. Available online at http://www.usnews.com/usnews/news/articles/961125/archive_035028.htm.

163. Ibid.

164. Ibid.

165. "Marching Side by Side," OnLine News Hour with Jim Lehrer, April 30, 1997. Available online at http://www.pbs.org/newshour/bb/military/april97/coed_4-30.html.

166. Zimmerman, *Tailspin*, pp. 161–162.

RESOURCES ///////

Books

Barkalow, Carol, with Andrea Raab. *In the Men's House: An Inside Account of Life in the Army by One of West Point's First Female Graduates.* New York: Poseidon Press, 1990.

Becraft, Carolyn. *Women in the U.S. Armed Services: The War in the Persian Gulf.* Washington, D.C.: Women's Research and Education Institute, 1991.

Blacksmith, E.A., ed. *Women in the Military.* New York: H. W. Wilson, 1992.

Blanton, De Ann, and Lauren M. Cook. *They Fought Like Demons: Women Soldiers in the Civil War.* New York: Vintage, 2003.

Binkin, Martin, and Shirley J. Bach. *Women and the Military.* Washington, D.C.: The Brookings Institution, 1977.

Bragg, Rick. *I Am a Soldier, Too: The Jessica Lynch Story.* New York: Knopf, 2003.

Brodie, Laura Fairchild. *Breaking Out: VMI and the Coming of Women.* New York: Vintage, 2001.

Buckley, Kevin. *Panama: The Whole Story.* New York: Simon & Schuster, 1991.

Chafe, William H. *The American Woman: Her Changing Social, Economic, and Political Roles, 1920–1970.* New York: Oxford University Press, 1972.

Clayton, Susan D., and Faye J. Crosby. *Justice, Gender, and Affirmative Action.* Ann Arbor, Mich.: University of Michigan Press, 1992.

Cornum, Rhonda, with Peter Copeland. *She Went to War: The Rhonda Cornum Story.* San Francisco: Presidio Press, 1992.

DePauw, Linda Grant. *Battle Cries and Lullabies: Women in War From Prehistory to the Present.* Norman: University of Oklahoma Press, 1998.

———. *The First Enlisted Women, 1917–1918.* Philadelphia: Dorrance and Co., 1955.

Ebbert, Jean, and Marie-Beth Hall. *Crossed Currents: Navy Women from WWI to Tailhook.* Washington, D.C.: Brassey's, 1993.

Flynn, George Q. *The Draft, 1940–1973.* Kansas City: University Press of Kansas, 1993.

Francke, Linda Bird. *Ground Zero: The Gender Wars in the Military.* New York: Simon & Schuster, 1997.

Fraser, Antonia. *The Warrior Queens.* New York: Knopf, 1989.

Gluck, Sherna Berger. *Rosie the Riveter Revisited: Women, the War, and Social Change.* Boston: Twayne Publishers, 1987.

Godson, Susan H. *Serving Proudly: A History of Women in the U.S. Navy.* Annapolis, Md.: Naval Institute Press, 2001.

Goldman, Nancy Loring, ed. *Female Soldiers: Combatants or Noncombatants?* Westport, Conn.: Greenwood Press, 1982.

Gruhzit-Hoyt, Olga. *They Also Served: American Women in World War II.* New York: Birch Lane Press Book, 1995.

Gutmann, Stephanie. *The Kinder, Gentler Military: Can America's Gender-Neutral Fighting Force Still Win Wars?* New York: Scribner, 2000.

Hayton-Keeva, Sally. *Valiant Women.* San Francisco: City Lights Books, 1987.

Holden, Henry M. *Ladybirds: The Untold Story of Women Pilots in America.* Seattle, Wash.: Black Hawk Press, 1991.

Holm, Major General Jeanne, USAF (Ret.) *Women in the Military: An Unfinished Revolution.* Revised ed. Novato, Calif.: Presidio Press, 1992.

Isaksson, Eve, ed. *Women and the Military System.* New York: St. Martin's Press, 1988.

Jones, David E. *Women Warriors: A History.* Washington, D.C.: Potomac Books, 1997.

Karsten, Peter. *Recruiting, Drafting, and Enlisting.* New York: Garland, 1998.

Laffin, John. *Women in Battle.* London: Abelard-Shuman, 1967.

Lyne, Mary C., and Kay Arthur. *Three Years behind the Mast: The Story of the United States Coast Guard SPARS.* Washington, D.C.: n.p., 1946.

Mace, Nancy, with Mary Jane Ross. *In the Company of Men: A Woman at the Citadel.* New York: Simon & Schuster, 2001.

Marshall, Kathryn. *In the Combat Zone: An Oral History of American Women in Vietnam.* Boston: Little, Brown, 1987.

Mezey, Susan Glick. *In Pursuit of Equality: Women, Public Policy, and Federal Courts.* New York: St. Martin's Press, 1992.

Mitchell, Brian. *Women in the Military: Flirting With Disaster.* Washington, D.C.: Regnery, 1998.

Oelke, Marion E. *Women in Combat Roles: Past and Future.* Maxwell Air Force Base, Ala.: Air War College, 1988.

Saywell, Shelley. *Women in War.* New York: Viking, 1985.

Schneider, Dorothy, and Carl J. Schneider. *Sound Off! American Military Women Speak Out.* New York: Paragon House, 1992.

Seeley, Charlotte P., ed. *American Women and the U.S. Armed Forces: A Guide to the Records of Military Agencies in the National Archives Relating* to *American Women.* Washington, D.C.: National Archives and Records Administration, 1992.

Stiehm, Judith Hicks. *Bring Me Men & Women: Mandated Change at the U.S. Air Force Academy.* San Francisco: University of California Press, 1981.

Stiehm, Judith Hicks, ed. *It's Our Military Too!: Women and the U.S. Military.* Philadelphia: Temple University, 1996.

Stremlow, Mary. *A History of the Women Marines, 1946–1977.* Washington, D.C.: U.S. Marine Corps, 1986.

Weatherford, Doris. *American Women and World War II.* New York: Facts On File, 1990.

Williams, Christine L. *Gender Differences at Work: Women and Men in Nontraditional Occupations.* Berkeley and Los Angeles: University of California Press, 1989.

Zimmerman, Jean. *Tailspin: Women at War in the Wake of Tailhook.* New York: Doubleday, 1995.

Articles and Reports

Anderson, James H., PhD. "Boot Camp or Summer Camp? Restoring Rigorous Standards to Basic Training." The Heritage Foundation, November 6, 1997. Available online at http://www.heritage.org/Research/PoliticalPhilosophy/BG1147.cfm.

Campbell, D'Ann. "Women in Combat: The World War Two Experience in the United States, Great Britain, Germany, and the Soviet Union." *Journal of Military History* (April 1993): pp. 301–323. Available online at http://members.aol.com/DAnn01/combat.html.

"Coed Training a Challenge in S.C.," *USA Today,* September 15, 1997, p. A18.

Gutmann, Stephanie. "Sex and the Soldier," *The New Republic,* February 24, 1997, p. 19.

"Marines Still Do It Their Way," *Time,* August 4, 1997.

Moskos, Charles C. "Female GIs in the Field," *Society,* September/October 1985, pp. 28–33.

Presidential Commission on the Assignment of Women in the Armed Services Report to the President. Washington, D.C.: U.S. Government Printing Office, 1993.

Priest, Dana. "Army Finds Wide Abuses of Women," *The Washington Post,* September 12, 1997, p. A1.

Sagawa, Shirley, and Nancy Duff Campbell. "Sexual Harassment of Women in the Military" (Issue Paper). Washington, D.C.: National Women's Law Center, 1992.

Secretary of the Army. *Senior Review Panel Report on Sexual Harassment.* Vol. 2, July 1997.

"Single-Sex Training Is Best for Men and Women," *Air Force Times*, June 9, 1997, p. 28.

Streich, Daniel B. "Perils of a Co-Ed Military," *The Washington Times*, June 29, 1997, p. B5.

Thomas, Patricia J., and J.E. Edwards. *Incidence of Pregnancy and Single Parenthood Among Enlisted Personnel in the Navy.* San Diego, Calif.: Navy Personnel Research and Development Center, 1989.

Thomas, Patricia J., and Marie D. Thomas. *Impact of Pregnant Women and Single Parents Upon Navy Personnel Systems.* San Diego, Calif.: Navy Personnel Research and Development Center, 1992.

Thompson, Mark. "Boot Camp Goes Soft," *Time,* August 4, 1997, p. 22.

Treadwell, Mattie E. U.S. *Army in World War II: Special Studies—The Women's Army Corps.* Washington, D.C.: Department of the Army, 1954.

USARIEM. "Incidence of and Risk Factors for Injury and Illness Among Male and Female Army Basic Trainees." USARIEM Report No. T19, 1988.

U.S. General Accounting Office. *Women in the Military—Deployment in the Persian Gulf War.* GAO/NSIAD-92-93, July 1993.

U.S. House Committee on Armed Services, Military Personnel and Compensation Subcommittee. *Parenting Issues of Operation Desert Storm: Hearing.* 102nd Congress, February 19, 1991.

Williams, Rudi. "Military Women Take 200-Year Trek Toward Respect, Parity." U.S. Department of Defense: American Forces Press Service, August 12, 1998. Available online at http://www.defenselink.mil/news/Aug1998/n08121998_9808123.html.

Women in Combat: Report to the President. The Presidential Commission on the Assignment of Women in the Armed Forces. 1992.

Web sites

Army Times

www.ArmyTimes.com
Weekly news service featuring articles of interest to people in the military.

Center for Military Readiness (CMR)

www.cmrlink.org
The Center for Military Readiness is an independent, non-partisan educational organization formed to take a leadership role in promoting sound military personnel policies in the armed forces. CMR is a group of civilian, active duty and retired military people in all 50 states that concentrates on military personnel issues full-time.

Defense Department Advisory Committee on Women in the Services (DACOWITS)

http://www.dtic.mil/dacowits
Established in 1951, DACOWITS is composed of civilian women and men who are appointed by the Secretary of Defense to provide advice and recommendations on matters and policies relating to the recruitment and retention, treatment, employment, integration, and well-being of highly qualified professional women in the Armed Forces.

Military Women "Firsts"

http://userpages.aug.com/captbarb/firsts.html
This Web site compiles a list of firsts for women in the military, including the first woman to enlist in each of the service branches, the first to receive various medals, and more.

The Minerva Center

http://www.minervacenter.com
Nonprofit educational foundation providing information about women in the military.

Legislation

Public Law 80-625

Known as the Women's Armed Services Integration Act of 1948, this law established the Women's Army Corps in the Regular Army and authorized the enlistment and appointment of women in the regular Air Force, regular Navy and Marine Corps, and in the Reserve components of the Army, Navy, Air Force, and Marine Corps. It also contained provisions that excluded women from combat assignments in the military (the so-called combat exclusionary laws). (United States Statutes at Large. Public Law 80-625, 80th Congress, 2d Session. Washington, D.C.: U.S. Government Printing Office, 1948.)

Executive Order 10240

Signed in 1951, this order permitted military officials to involuntarily discharge women from the military if the women were pregnant or responsible for minor children (as mothers, stepmothers, or foster parents).

Equal Employment Opportunity Commission (EEOC) (1964)

This commission was established by Title VII of the Civil Rights Act of 1964 to enforce provisions that related to bans on discrimination because of race, color, religion, national origin, or gender.

Public Law 90-130

This law lifted the 2 percent ceiling on the number of women in the military and made women in the Army, Navy, Air Force, and Marine Corps eligible for promotion to flag rank. It also eliminated arbitrary ceilings on the number of women who could reach certain middle grades. This law was the first major policy change regarding women in the U.S. military since 1948. (United States Statutes at Large: Public Law 90-130, Washington, D.C.: U.S. Government Printing Office, 1967.)

Public Law 94-106; Section 803(a)

Signed into law in 1975, this act declared that women would be eligible for appointment and admission to the nation's military academies, including the United States Military Academy (West Point), the United States Naval Academy, and the United States Air Force Academy, beginning with the class that entered in calendar year 1976. It further declared that "academic and other relevant standards required for appointment, admission, training, graduation, and commissioning of female individuals shall be the same as those required for male individuals, except for those minimum essential adjustments in such standards required because of physiological differences between male and female individuals."

Public Law 95-202

In 1977, Congress passed this law to accord veteran status to women who had served as members of the Signal Corps during World War I.

Pregnancy Discrimination Act (PDA) of 1978

This amendment to Title VII of the Civil Rights Act of 1964 added pregnancy to the list of areas in which people might face discrimination on the basis of gender. It bans discriminating against women because of pregnancy, childbirth, or related medical conditions.

Title 10 USC 6015

In 1978, this act, which banned women from being assigned to seagoing vessels other than certain hospital and rescue ships, was amended to permit women on noncombatant ships.

Defense Officer Manpower Personnel Management Act (1980)

This act authorized a single personnel system with integrated lists of male and female personnel for appointments and promotions. As a result, male and female officers compete with each other for positions in the services.

Direct Combat Probability Coding (DCPC) (1982)

The Army developed this tool for identifying which positions would be closed to women. It states that women cannot be assigned to positions that are likely to place them in direct combat situations. Rankings from P1 to P7 are assigned to each position in the Army. The lower the number, the greater the risk; thus, all positions labeled P1 have been closed to women.

Department of Defense Risk Rule (1988)

Under this rule, the service branches were required to set standard rules for determining how women could serve in various roles. It permitted the services to exclude women from noncombatant positions that involved "risks of exposure to direct combat, hostile fire, or capture [if] such risks are equal to or greater than that experienced by associated combat units in the same theater of operations."

Public Law 103-160

With the passage of this law, Secretary of Defense Les Aspin notified Congress of "Proposed Changes in Combat Assignments to Which Female Members May Be Assigned," opening many new positions for women, especially in the air force and navy (United States Statutes at Large. Public Law 103-160, 103d Congress. Washington, D.C.: U.S. Government Printing Office, 1993.)

Public Law 102-190

This law repealed statutory limitations that previously banned assigning women in the armed forces to combat aircraft. (United States Statutes at Large. Public Law 102-190, 102nd Congress, 1st session. Washington, D.C.: U.S. Government. Printing Office, 1991.)

Public Law 103-160

This law repealed statutory restrictions that had excluded women from certain assignments on seagoing ships in the Navy and Marine Corps. (United States Statutes at Large. Public Law 103-160, 103d Congress. Washington, D.C.: U.S. Government Printing Office, 1993.)

Kennedy-Roth Amendment (to the Defense Authorizations Act, FY 1992–93)

This amendment repealed provisions of Title 10 USC 8549 that banned women from serving on combat aircraft engaged in combat missions.

Title 10 USC 6015

Repealed in 1994, this act once banned women from being assigned to naval combatant ships.

Title 10, U.S.C. 3012

This law gives the secretary of the army authority to determine personnel policy for the Army and provides the basis for policies that exclude women from serving in units that are likely to be involved in direct ground combat.

Public Law 103-446

In 1994, this law established the Center for Women Veterans within the Department for Veteran's Affairs.

The Department of Defense issued a formal definition of sexual assault in 2004. It says, in part, that:

- Sexual assault is a crime. It is defined as intentional sexual contact, characterized by use of force, physical threat or abuse of authority or when the victim does not or cannot consent.

- Sexual assault includes rape, nonconsensual sodomy (oral or anal sex), indecent assault (unwanted, inappropriate sexual contact or fondling), or attempts to commit these acts.

- Sexual assault can occur without regard to gender or spousal relationship or age of victim.

- "Consent" shall not be deemed or construed to mean the failure by the victim to offer physical resistance. Consent is not given when a person uses force, threat of force, coercion or when the victim is asleep, incapacitated, or unconscious.

Cases

Owens v. Brown, 455 F. Supp. 291, 200 (D.D.C. 1978)

Yona Owens, a member of the Navy who worked as an interior communications electrician, filed a class action suit on behalf of herself and other women who sought the opportunity to serve on board oceangoing vessels. They challenged Title 10 USC 6015, saying that it discriminated unfairly on the basis of gender and denied them equal protection under the laws. District Court Judge John J. Sirica ruled in favor of Owens on July 27, 1978, striking down Section 6015 on the grounds that it denied women as a group equal protection. As a result, women in the Navy were considered for sea duty.

Frontiero v. Richardson, 411 U.S. 677 (1973)

Sharron A. Frontiero, a physical therapist in the Air Force, filed a suit that alleged sexual discrimination because military policies did not regard her husband as a dependent, although it did regard all wives of servicemen as dependents. Servicewomen were required to show that they provided at least half of their spouse's support. As a result of this policy, Frontiero was not eligible for economical on-base housing and her husband was denied health care benefits. The U.S. Supreme Court ruled in her favor, stating that the dependents of women in the military were entitled to the same benefits as the dependents of male servicemen. The court said that any special burdens of proof placed on servicewomen regarding civilian spouses must also apply to servicemen.

Crawford v. Cushman, 531 F. 2d 1114 (2d Cir. 1976)
A U.S. Court of Appeals struck down a Marine regulation that mandated discharging women because of pregnancy, saying that this policy violated a woman's right to due process and equal protection under the laws.

Rostker v. Goldberg, 453 U.S. 57 (1981)
The U.S. Supreme Court upheld the constitutionality of requiring only men to register with the Selective Service system. The court said that the armed forces can use this gender-based classification system as part of its process for deciding how to enlist and assign personnel in the most effective way.

Faulkner v. The Citadel, 51 F.3d 440, 233 (4th Cir. 1995)
Shannon Faulkner sued The Citadel, a state-supported military college in South Carolina, when it refused to admit her to its Corps of Cadets but instead offered to let her attend day classes. The court ruled that Faulkner was entitled to attend the school on the same terms as male students, based on the Fourteenth Amendment's guarantee of "equal protection of the laws." The Citadel was ordered to admit Faulkner and to formulate and implement a plan for other women to attend the school beginning in fall 1995.

United States v. Virginia et al., 518 U.S. 515 (1996)
The U.S. Supreme Court confirmed a ruling by the Court of Appeals for the 4th Circuit that stated that the male-only admission policy at Virginia Military Institute (VMI) violated women applicants right to equal protection under the Fourteenth Amendment. VMI had proposed placing women in a parallel program at a nearby women's college, but the court declared that this program was not equal in terms of the course offerings or qualifications of the faculty.

Terms and Concepts

all-volunteer force
collocation
combat exclusion laws
combat readiness
deployability
direct combat
direct combat probability code
discrimination
draft laws
equal opportunity
exclusionary policies

fraternization
gender-integrated basic training
  (GIBT)
ground combat
"lost time"
mixed-gender units (also: gender-
  integrated units)
military readiness
Risk Rule
sexual harassment
sexual misconduct

Beginning Legal Research

The goal of POINT/COUNTERPOINT is not only to provide the reader with an introduction to a controversial issue affecting society, but also to encourage the reader to explore the issue more fully. This appendix, then, is meant to serve as a guide to the reader in researching the current state of the law as well as exploring some of the public-policy arguments as to why existing laws should be changed or new laws are needed.

Like many types of research, legal research has become much faster and more accessible with the invention of the Internet. This appendix discusses some of the best starting points, but of course "surfing the Net" will uncover endless additional sources of information—some more reliable than others. Some important sources of law are not yet available on the Internet, but these can generally be found at the larger public and university libraries. Librarians usually are happy to point patrons in the right direction.

The most important source of law in the United States is the Constitution. Originally enacted in 1787, the Constitution outlines the structure of our federal government and sets limits on the types of laws that the federal government and state governments can pass. Through the centuries, a number of amendments have been added to or changed in the Constitution, most notably the first ten amendments, known collectively as the Bill of Rights, which guarantee important civil liberties. Each state also has its own constitution, many of which are similar to the U.S. Constitution. It is important to be familiar with the U.S. Constitution because so many of our laws are affected by its requirements. State constitutions often provide protections of individual rights that are even stronger than those set forth in the U.S. Constitution.

Within the guidelines of the U.S. Constitution, Congress—both the House of Representatives and the Senate—passes bills that are either vetoed or signed into law by the President. After the passage of the law, it becomes part of the United States Code, which is the official compilation of federal laws. The state legislatures use a similar process, in which bills become law when signed by the state's governor. Each state has its own official set of laws, some of which are published by the state and some of which are published by commercial publishers. The U.S. Code and the state codes are an important source of legal research; generally, legislators make efforts to make the language of the law as clear as possible.

However, reading the text of a federal or state law generally provides only part of the picture. In the American system of government, after the legislature passes laws and the executive (U.S. President or state governor) signs them, it is up to the judicial branch of the government, the court system, to interpret the laws and decide whether they violate any provision of the Constitution. At the state level, each state's supreme court has the ultimate authority in determining what a law means and whether or not it violates the state constitution. However, the federal courts—headed by the U.S. Supreme Court—can review state laws and court decisions to determine whether they violate federal laws or the U.S. Constitution. For example, a state court may find that a particular criminal law is valid under the state's constitution, but a federal court may then review the state court's decision and determine that the law is invalid under the U.S. Constitution.

It is important, then, to read court decisions when doing legal research. The Constitution uses language that is intentionally very general—for example, prohibiting "unreasonable searches and seizures" by the police—and court cases often provide more guidance. For example, the U.S. Supreme Court's 2001 decision in *Kyllo* v. *United States* held that scanning the outside of a person's house using a heat sensor to determine whether the person is growing marijuana is unreasonable—*if* it is done without a search warrant secured from a judge. Supreme Court decisions provide the most definitive explanation of the law of the land, and it is therefore important to include these in research. Often, when the Supreme Court has not decided a case on a particular issue, a decision by a federal appeals court or a state supreme court can provide guidance; but just as laws and constitutions can vary from state to state, so can federal courts be split on a particular interpretation of federal law or the U.S. Constitution. For example, federal appeals courts in Louisiana and California may reach opposite conclusions in similar cases.

Lawyers and courts refer to statutes and court decisions through a formal system of citations. Use of these citations reveals which court made the decision (or which legislature passed the statute) and when and enables the reader to locate the statute or court case quickly in a law library. For example, the legendary Supreme Court case *Brown* v. *Board of Education* has the legal citation 347 U.S. 483 (1954). At a law library, this 1954 decision can be found on page 483 of volume 347 of the U.S. Reports, the official collection of the Supreme Court's decisions. Citations can also be helpful in locating court cases on the Internet.

Understanding the current state of the law leads only to a partial under-standing of the issues covered by the POINT/COUNTERPOINT series. For a fuller understanding of the issues, it is necessary to look at public-policy arguments claiming that the current state of the law is not adequately addressing the issue.

Many groups lobby for new legislation or changes to existing legislation; the National Rifle Association (NRA), for example, lobbies Congress and the state legislatures constantly to make existing gun control laws less restrictive and not to pass additional laws. The NRA and other groups dedicated to various causes might also intervene in pending court cases: a group such as Planned Parenthood might file a brief *amicus curiae* (as "a friend of the court")—called an "amicus brief"—in a lawsuit that could affect abortion rights. Interest groups also use the media to influence public opinion, issuing press releases and frequently appearing in interviews on news programs and talk shows. The books in POINT/COUNTERPOINT list some of the interest groups that are active in the issue at hand, but in each case there are countless other groups working at the local, state, and national levels. It is important to read everything with a critical eye, for sometimes interest groups present information in a way that can be read only to their advantage. The informed reader must always look for bias.

Finding sources of legal information on the Internet is relatively simple thanks to "portal" sites such as FindLaw (*www.findlaw.com*), which provides access to a variety of constitutions, statutes, court opinions, law review articles, news articles, and other resources—including all Supreme Court decisions issued since 1893. Other useful sources of information include the U.S. Government Printing Office (*www.gpo.gov*), which contains a complete copy of the U.S. Code, and the Library of Congress's THOMAS system (*thomas.loc.gov*), which offers access to bills pending before Congress as well as recently passed laws. Of course, the Internet changes every second of every day, so it is best to do some independent searching. Most cases, studies, and opinions that are cited or referred to in public debate can be found online—and *everything* can be found in one library or another.

The Internet can provide a basic understanding of most important legal issues, but not all sources can be found there. To find some documents it is necessary to visit the law library of a university or a public law library; some cities have public law libraries, and many library systems keep legal documents at the main branch. On the following page are some common citation forms.

COMMON CITATION FORMS

Source of Law	Sample Citation	Notes
U.S. Supreme Court	*Employment Division v. Smith*, 485 U.S. 660 (1988)	The U.S. Reports is the official record of Supreme Court decisions. There is also an unofficial Supreme Court ("S. Ct.") reporter.
U.S. Court of Appeals	*United States v. Lambert*, 695 F.2d 536 (11th Cir.1983)	Appellate cases appear in the Federal Reporter, designated by "F." The 11th Circuit has jurisdiction in Alabama, Florida, and Georgia.
U.S. District Court	*Carillon Importers, Ltd. v. Frank Pesce Group, Inc.*, 913 F.Supp. 1559 (S.D.Fla.1996)	Federal trial-level decisions are reported in the Federal Supplement ("F. Supp."). Some states have multiple federal districts; this case originated in the Southern District of Florida.
U.S. Code	Thomas Jefferson Commemoration Commission Act, 36 U.S.C., §149 (2002)	Sometimes the popular names of legislation—names with which the public may be familiar—are included with the U.S. Code citation.
State Supreme Court	*Sterling v. Cupp*, 290 Ore. 611, 614, 625 P.2d 123, 126 (1981)	The Oregon Supreme Court decision is reported in both the state's reporter and the Pacific regional reporter.
State Statute	Pennsylvania Abortion Control Act of 1982, 18 Pa. Cons. Stat. 3203-3220 (1990)	States use many different citation formats for their statutes.

INDEX

PICTURE CREDITS /|/|//|//

page:

19: Library of Congress, LC-USZC4-1653

22: Associated Press

37: Courtesy of the Department of Defense

47: AP Images/Spc. Jeremy D. Crisp

67: Courtesy of the Department of Defense

70: AP Images/LM Otero

77: Courtesy of the Department of Defense

109: Courtesy of the Marine Corps

cover: Courtesy of the Department of Defense

VICTORIA SHERROW is a freelance writer and member of the Society of Children's Book Writers. She is also the author of many books for middle- and high-school readers, including *Great Scientists,* and *Political Leaders and Peacemakers.*

ALAN MARZILLI, M.A., J.D., lives in Washington, D.C., and is a program associate with Advocates for Human Potential, Inc., a research and consulting firm based in Sudbury, Mass., and Albany, N.Y. He primarily works on developing training and educational materials for agencies of the federal government on topics such as housing, mental health policy, employment, and transportation. He has spoken on mental health issues in 30 states, the District of Columbia, and Puerto Rico; his work has included training mental health administrators, nonprofit management and staff, and people with mental illnesses and their families on a wide variety of topics, including effective advocacy, community-based mental health services, and housing. He has written several handbooks and training curricula that are used nationally and as far away as the territory of Guam. He managed statewide and national mental health advocacy programs and worked for several public interest lobbying organizations while studying law at Georgetown University. He has written more than a dozen books, including numerous titles in the *Point/Counterpoint* series.